What matters most of All

The Seed Was Always There

**IMPACTFUL STORIES
FROM TWO WOMEN PASTORS**

Lucy Kyllonen & Lena Meadowcroft

Copyright © 2018 by NOW SC Press

All rights reserved. No part of this publication may be reproduced, distributed, or transmitted in any form or by any means, including photocopying, recording, or other electronic or mechanical methods, without the prior written permission of the publisher, except in the case of brief quotations embodied in critical reviews and certain other noncommercial uses permitted by copyright law. For permission requests, write to the publisher, addressed "Attention: Permissions Coordinator," via the website below.

1.888.5069-NOW
www.nowscpress.com
@nowscpress

Ordering Information:

Quantity sales. Special discounts are available on quantity purchases by corporations, associations, and others. For details, contact the publisher at the address above.

Orders by U.S. trade bookstores and wholesalers. Please contact: NOW SC Press: Tel: (888) 5069-NOW or visit www.nowscpress.com.

Printed in the United States of America

First Printing, 2018

ISBN: 978-0-9987391-8-2

Dedications

I am extremely grateful to God for allowing me the opportunity to witness such amazing testimonies from both near and far, and to be able to share the impact with so many others. My dedication is to all the fearless people who made the stories in this book possible. Your journeys may have been difficult but God is using them to inspire and encourage us all.

—Lucy

For my parents, James and Ruby. Thank you for teaching me to always trust and rely on Jesus and for supporting all my crazy ideas! I love you both!

—Lena

Contents

Introduction 1
Forgiveness 3
Pride 11
Yourself 21
Joy 29
Loss 37
Self-Reliance 45
Acceptance 55
Success 63
Control 71
Anger 79
Faith 87
Change 95
Compassion 103
Relationships 111
Insecurity 119
Failure 127
Guilt & Shame 135
Fear 143
About the Authors 151

Introduction

Thank you for reading along with us! We hope the stories in this book inspire you and give you room to pause and think. So many of us struggle in our walk with the Lord, particularly when life throws us curveballs. The stories in this book are designed to show you that you are not alone in your struggles and that others have been there and triumphed.

The title of this book, *The Seed Was Always There*, means that the seed of your faith is there inside you already. All it takes is a little nurturing and connection to grow it and build a stronger foundation with the Lord. We hope that you can use the referenced verses and lessons to draw closer to God.

Finally, we have included questions for reflection. You can use these any way you like—to think about after you read that day's passage, to discuss with a close friend or in a study/connect group, or to journal about in your devotional time. Use them as a springboard to examine your faith and enrich your relationship with Christ.

Most of all, we hope you find a message of hope and strength in these pages, and that each story helps you grow that seed of faith into a strong, well-rooted tree.

Pastor Lucy and Pastor Lena

** Unless otherwise noted, all Bible verses are from NIV (New International Version) or ESV (English Standard Version).

Forgiveness

"Bear with each other and forgive one another if any of you has a grievance against someone. Forgive as the Lord forgave you."

Colossians 3:13

—Pastor Lucy

Forgiving the unforgivable.

The woman across from me told me a painful, horrific story in a soft, low voice. She paused and then said, "I need to do something that I needed to do a long time ago. Offering him forgiveness will be one of the hardest things I've ever had to do." She looked up at me. "I'm scared."

I understood her fear. Forgiving what seems unforgiveable requires a massive amount of fortitude and faith. But my friend, who exposed layer after layer of her past during our conversation, was one of the strongest people I'd ever met.

Marie was born and raised in California. When she was seven years old, the man who was supposed to protect her, her father, began sexually abusing her. All the innocence that rightly belonged to her was forcefully stripped away. She confided in her mother, expecting refuge and support. Instead, her mother betrayed her, telling Marie to hide this secret and never speak of it again. With her silence, the abuse got worse sending Marie into a downward spiral.

Why We Need Forgiveness

We have all been hurt by the words or actions of others. **The worst sting is when that hurt comes from someone we love.** A wounded heart can leave us with years of anger, bitterness, and resentment, along with an occasional burning desire for vengeance. Although we may never forget the hurt that was done to us, it is possible to break away from the hold it has on our lives and prevent it from causing any more damage.

Jesus is the ultimate example of forgiveness. He loved and He forgave, over and over again. There's a dramatic story in the Bible, found in John, chapter 8, where the Temple leaders brought what they thought would be a challenging issue to Jesus. A woman was caught in the act of adultery, an offense punishable by death—stoning to death to be exact. The Temple leaders brought her before Him expecting justice to be done—not only for her betrayed husband, but also for every man he represented. As this was a capital punishment, a curious crowd gathered to watch. To everyone's surprise, Jesus stood up and, without speaking a word, began writing in the sand. That was unusual. Finally, He spoke and when He did, He said, "Let he who is without sin cast the first stone." Perplexed and confused, the crowd dissipated, dropping their stones to the ground. Then He gently told the offender, "Go and sin no more." In this story, Jesus does not condemn the woman for her actions. Instead, she is called to change. He calls her to repentance but the message here is for each and every one of us.

You may find this astonishing, but we need to forgive our offender. Even if he or she instigated our downward spiral. For Marie, what her father did to her led to defiant behavior well into her thirties. In her teens, she was introduced to the world of drugs and alcohol. For her, those substances masked her pain and provided temporary respite, allowing her to forget about the abuse. Eventually, her past made its way back into her reality. Its strong grip was forcing out any goodness she had left in her. She found herself in a jail cell for domestic violence, not once, not twice, but three times. By that point, she'd become consumed by the anger she felt for her father's actions. Someone had to pay and hurt just like she did.

It's so easy for us to point the finger at others when we have been wronged. As much as we wish it didn't, evil exists and runs rampant in this world. Sin is destructive. Yet, when Peter asked Jesus if he had to forgive people up to seven times, Peter was surprised by His response. "Jesus answered, 'I tell you, not seven times, but seventy-seven times.'" (Matthew 18:22) The message here, however, goes beyond numerical value. Jesus paints a picture of a lifestyle of forgiveness. Even in the most difficult situations, He tells us to forgive. Even if you are the one who has been wronged, forgive. Even if you don't feel like it, forgive. It really is for your own good.

There's an old saying that goes: Holding onto unforgiveness or anger is like drinking poison and expecting the other person to die.

When we choose not to forgive others it jeopardizes our walk with God. Forgiving releases anger and hurt and allows us to receive all the healing that God has for us. In Colossians, we are told we must learn to develop a heart and attitude of forgiveness so that the Father will forgive us of our own sins (verse 13). We do this by putting on a new nature and being renewed as we learn how to become more like Christ (verse10). The message of Christ has to fill our lives (verse16) and everything we do should be done for the Lord, rather than people (verse 23). Forgiving others becomes easier the more you practice it and realize that it is Christ in you who empowers you to do what seems impossible. In return, we receive His undeserving forgiveness, mercy, and grace when we seek atonement for our own wrongs.

When Healing Takes Place

Something peculiar happened the last time Marie found herself in jail. A lady approached her and asked Marie if she could pray Psalm 23 and anoint her head with oil. Marie had no idea what that meant but she consented. Little did she know how that prayer would change her life. In that moment, the woman introduced Marie to Jesus, the Good Shepherd, and all He has to offer: rest, protection, comfort, blessings, and goodness all the days of her life. From that day forward, transformation began taking place in Marie's life and heart. A bed opened up at a rehabilitation center that previously hadn't had room. Marie spent three months there, freeing herself from the chains of drugs and alcohol. God was at work behind the scenes. While she was at the rehabilitation center, a halfway house for women offered her a bed, something most people don't get for months. In that moment, the woman and Psalm 23 turned Marie's life around one hundred and eighty degrees—she has never gone back to that life and her joy for God is contagious.

If you were fortunate enough to meet Marie today, you would have no idea what she went through. Instead, you would meet someone who is passionate, full of life, and a devoted follower of Jesus. She's happily married and has grown children who have blessed her with grandkids. She's involved in her home church, giving of herself and her resources, and she recently purchased a home in the community for women who have been victimized by the sex industry.

Life is not fair. We all know that, but you have a choice in how you deal with the challenges and wrongs in your life. If you stay wrapped up in pain and anger, you'll never be able to fully experience or enjoy the present. Forgiveness is a process, one that requires a commitment to personal change. Forgiveness does not guarantee or require reconciliation, nor does it condone the offense. Forgiveness isn't about the offender—it's about you and your relationship with God. Forgiveness takes more courage than choosing not to forgive or let go and it allows you to hope for the future. Marie knew this, but also understood that, through forgiveness, the gift she would receive forever outweighed her fear.

As I listened to her speak, I was amazed by her bravery and inspired by her story. Marie had forgiven her father and, in turn, asked her to forgive him. Marie moved on and began working to heal the wound of her mother's silence all these years. She talked to her mother and they reconciled. In the end, Marie's act of forgiveness wasn't weakness—it was an act of incredible strength.

Questions for Reflection

1. What is your initial reaction regarding a lifestyle of forgiveness?

2. How does our unwillingness to forgive result in a victim mentality?

3. As Christians, how should we deal with people who continually offend us?

4. If you have experienced a significant forgiveness incident, what steps did you take and what helped you heal from it?

Pride

God opposes the proud but gives grace to the humble.

James 4:6

—*Pastor Lena*

At a church service I attended many years ago, I heard a family tell a story about pride. I was blown away by the impact of their powerful message: God's plans for the Harrison family were nearly destroyed by their pride.

Money Isn't Everything

When John Harrison left the military, he started a job selling cleaning products door to door. He was an exceptional salesman and was quickly promoted, becoming an area manager with several employees working for him. John eventually bought his own franchise of the business, and he and his wife worked hard to build a multimillion dollar company. They lived in the comforts of one of the exclusive upscale neighborhoods in Fort Lauderdale, Florida. Their wealth and success earned them the traditional millionaire toys—luxury cars, expensive handbags, diamond jewelry, priceless artwork, and extravagant vacations. They were living "the American Dream".

During a visit with a customer, Jane Harrison had a truly life-changing experience. While chatting, the woman shared the message of Jesus with her. Jane found the message so powerful she surrendered her heart to the Lord, asking for forgiveness and accepting Jesus into her heart. She left that fateful meeting full of hope but longing for more. The minute she got home, Jane shared her experience with her husband but he was not as excited by the encounter.

Jane held on to the experience and began to make drastic changes in her life. She took time off work, going to conferences and traveling around the world to hear different ministers speak and teach about Jesus. At a revival in Louisiana, one full of singing, clapping, and preaching, Jane's life was forever changed. The revival service was led by a minister from Africa, and after four hours of preaching God's word he asked people to line up and receive prayer. Jane stood in line, expecting God to do something in her heart that He had never done before. After all, the man had preached about feeling God's presence in a tangible way and she had read stories of people receiving miracles and healing in their bodies.

The preacher reached out, grabbed her by the hand, and started praying. In that moment, Jane felt the most incredible heat go into her hand and shoot through her whole body. **She said it was hot yet comforting, as if God Himself had engulfed her in a warm blanket.** She left that meeting feeling different, as if her skin was new. She felt clean, as if whatever that sensation was had burned off the sins in her life.

Jane had felt God's overwhelming love and it changed her in fundamental ways. She immediately got on the phone with her husband, who was working at home in south Florida. She tried to describe what happened during the prayer but she couldn't get the words out because she was crying so hard. Concerned for his wife and wanting to know what happened, John flew out to join her the following day. As soon as the revival service started, John swore he felt rain, as if a total downpour had begun. Being from south Florida, he knew what it felt like for the skies to suddenly unleash a torrential rain where nothing was visible beyond five feet—a rain that hits the skin like pins and needles. However, when John opened his eyes he was completely dry, not a drop of water anywhere, yet he could still feel this downpour hitting him. John soon realized God was pouring out His presence and love on his body. When John later shared his story with the congregation, he said that was the night God told him to attend a Bible college and become a preacher.

John and his wife had only weeks to finalize their decision to attend Bible college. They sold their business and gave away much of the furniture and artwork in their home. Things that were once so precious, the spoils of their hard work, now seemed worthless. Their encounter with God during that revival service revealed to them how they had let worldly things—riches, notoriety, and business success—create a false sense of fulfillment. Their lives had become full of pride. **They allowed their achievements and possessions to define who they were**. God took away from the Harrisons the desire to be fulfilled by personal success and instead taught them to find fulfillment only in Jesus. The couple wanted to honor God with their lives, so when God directed them to go to Bible college, they listened and acted on His Word.

It took six weeks for the Harrisons to sell or give away their possessions and then they moved to refocus their lives. The couple spent the next three years learning about Jesus while attending a Bible college in west Florida. They went from their mansion near the beach to renting a tiny townhouse where the appliances barely worked. Instead of working traditional jobs, they served in the local church connected to the school. They volunteered for every position, whether that meant scrubbing toilets or packing boxes of food for the needy. When it neared time for them to complete their studies, God spoke to Jane, telling her to pack their bags and prepare to travel. She wasn't sure where they were going but she did as

God instructed. She purchased luggage, packed six suitcases for the two of them, renewed their passports, and set the suitcases by the front door.

A week after graduation, the church's pastor approached the Harrisons and asked about their future plans. The pastor had no idea of the Harrisons' business background, only knowing them as a faithful and reliable couple that had just completed college. He had watched them serve in different departments around the church. The pastor stunned them by asking, "Would you and your wife be willing to travel the country with me when I start preaching in other churches?" There it was! The very thing God spoke to Jane about was coming true. The couple spent the next five years traveling with the pastor throughout the U.S. and around the world. They were later offered salaried positions to run global missions for the church, overseeing a large staff of volunteers and missionaries. About ten years after setting upon their new paths, while running the church's missions department, the Harrisons reentered the business world and repurchased the franchise they once owned. The couple had learned not to let pride control their life, making God the center of every decision and surrendering their comfort for His purpose. The Harrisons learned that wealth gained through their own strengths lead only to pride, and once God saw their contentment with the little they had, **He rewarded them openly by giving back more than they could ever imagine.**

God Hates Pride

God is love. He loves everyone unconditionally, no matter where they are in life. However, there are things that God hates. Proverbs 6:16-19 lists the seven things God hates, and pride is first on the list. *"To fear the Lord is to hate evil; I hate pride and arrogance, evil behavior and perverse speech."* (Proverbs 8:13) God hates pride because it directly opposes the characteristics He wants people to strive for, to be humble, lowly, loving, trustworthy, meek, and God-fearing. Because it is opposed to God, pride is the root of all the evil that takes place. A prideful person loves money before God, has selfish ambition, and looks at their wealth as something acquired by their own hand, leaving God out of it.

The root of pride is found in every vice that is opposed to God. Vices like anger, sexual immorality, and drunkenness proclaim we don't need to follow the rules. They tell God, "I am my own person and I can do what I want, when I want—screw the consequences." James 4 tells us pride is rebellion towards God. It allows a person to be haughty of the things they do; living by their own rules and disregarding the rules God has already put in place for us. *"God opposes the proud but gives grace to the humble."* (James 4:6)

Before their life-changing experience at the revival, the Harrisons were good people who took care of their employees, but pride still ruled their lives.

The accolades and praise they received from their accomplishments and successes were theirs alone—not God's. They allowed pride to overshadow the blessings God gave them. The focus was on them and not on God. Their collections were their validation instead of God. There is a harsh warning against greed and pride in Deuteronomy, Chapter 8. God warns the people that He is the one taking care of them, providing all that they need, and that their great wealth is not anything they have done but is there because they are humbly serving Him. God warns not to deny all He does for them when they see their success as something they accomplished. God also warns people not to let pride overtake their lives to the point that they follow idols or false gods. God wants everyone to remember Him when it comes to success and wealth. "*But remember the Lord your God, for it is he who gives you the ability to produce wealth.* (Deuteronomy 8:18)

Pride comes in many forms. A person's pride may not be as obvious as the Harrisons'; few people have a million-dollar business and thousands of dollars worth of valuable items in their home. Pride can be a desire to be repeatedly praised for an accomplishment or believing you are better than other people. Have you looked down on a homeless person? Seen a disheveled woman and judged her? Made fun of someone who was handicapped or made a mistake? Those are all signs of pride, of thinking you are somehow better than another of God's precious creations.

The only way to overcome pride is to first ask forgiveness from God and He is always ready to do so. Once forgiven by God, people should seek forgiveness in one another. People must live humbly. Christ serves as an example of how to live a life of humility.

> *"In your relationships with one another, have the same mindset as Christ Jesus: Who, being in very nature God, did not consider equality with God something to be used to his own advantage; rather, he made himself nothing by taking the very nature of a servant, being made in human likeness. And being found in appearance as a man, he humbled himself by becoming obedient to death—even death on a cross!"*
>
> (Philippians 2:5-8)

> *"Humble yourselves before the Lord, and he will lift you up."*
>
> (James 4:10)

Jesus endured all these painful experiences so people can be exalted with Him. (Philippians 2:9-11) By following God's commands and being humble, people will find that they have no room in their hearts for pride.

Questions for Reflection

1. Why does God hate pride?
2. Can you identify where you may have pride?
3. Why do you think God exalts humble people?
4. Read Deuteronomy Chapter 8. What did God provide to the children of Israel?
5. Read Deuteronomy Chapter 8. What does God think about wealth?
6. Read James 4:1-6. James connects pride to people's vices and activities. Using James's definition of "lust", identify things in your life you lust for.

Yourself

*"Then you will know the truth,
and the truth will set you free.."*

John 8:32

—Pastor Lucy

Sabbatical.

The word literally means "ceasing", a period of rest or an extended absence from work in order to re-energize yourself; to allow for creative and new thinking, or to learn a new skill. I had been in the ministry for twenty years when I took a one-month sabbatical. I intended to use it as a long-overdue break from my never-ending work in ministry and catching up on my house chores. I made a detailed schedule, which included my devotions, spending some time with God, and a few days at the beach with the family. I was so excited to have this new freedom I could hardly contain myself! I was finally taking some time for myself and to spend some alone time with God. At least, that was my intent.

A few days later, I found myself flat on the ground in pain. After hanging the wash out on the line to dry, I casually lifted the laundry basket and felt a sharp pain in my lower back that left me gasping for breath. The slightest move caused intense pain. I knew what that meant—my back went out on me. I had thrown it out of alignment again. I wasn't surprised. I had been working so much that I was long overdue for my regularly scheduled appointment with my chiropractor. Once I got back into the house, I carefully and slowly positioned myself on the floor with my knees slightly elevated. I knew I needed to make an emergency appointment for and adjustment and that I'd be out of commission for at least a week as my back gradually healed. From my place on the floor, I cried out to God, *Why?*

Deep down, I already knew the answer. God meant for this to happen. I was getting in the way of experiencing what God wanted for me—a true ceasing, rest and restoration. The very thing I had asked for, prayed for, and anticipated, but the planner in me scheduled each day around long to-do lists. **My disobedience caused God to do something drastic to get my full attention—He forced me to rest, which was what I needed more than anything.**

Why Rest?

In Romans 7:18-20, the apostle Paul states, *"For I have the desire to do what is right, but not the ability to carry it out. For I do not do the good I want, but the evil I do not want is what I keep on doing. Now if I do what I do not want, it is no longer I who do it, but sin that dwells within me."* Sometimes, there is a strong divide between our will and our actions. I absolutely knew that if I didn't get back on track with my regular chiropractic appointments, my back would gradually become misaligned and cause great pain, leaving me unable to do the things I needed to do. Yet, I resisted what I knew to be right, the knowledge that God had given me. Instead I found myself barreling through warning signs and focusing on my to-do lists, focusing on myself and my world, instead of God's plan.

Like many of you, I'm sure, I really do want to do the right thing, but sometimes I can't or simply won't. **God gave us commandments to follow so that we can live life to the fullest according to His will.** Following His ways frees us to receive and experience all the blessings He has for us while here on earth. So, how does resting fit in to His plan and does it even work? How is it possible to rest when there is so much to do, so much to enjoy, so much to see and to experience? God managed to fit it in and He wants us to do the same. *"By the seventh day God had finished the work he had been doing; so on the seventh day he rested from all his work. Then God blessed the seventh* *day and made it holy, because on it he rested from all the work of creating that he had done."* (Genesis 2:2-3) The Sabbath was a part of creation. God didn't rest because He was tired or because He had to. On the day of rest, He celebrated His finished works.

He commands us to rest in Exodus 20:8-10: *"Remember the Sabbath day, to keep it holy. Six days you shall labor and do all your work, but the seventh day is a Sabbath to the Lord your God. On it you shall not do any work, neither you, nor your son or daughter, nor your male or female servant, or your livestock, or the sojourner who is within your gates."* I know this scripture and have read it a million times, but I resisted doing that because I didn't think it possible in the 21st century. I honored the Sabbath when I was able to schedule it in or when I found it convenient. When I considered setting aside a day to rest, I focused more on what I would be giving up—on how far behind it would put me, or how it would impact me. Do you see the common word there? *Me.* **I'd forgotten that it's God's plans for me, not my plans for myself that were important**. I'd been setting Him aside and was not freely enjoying what God has given me.

God made one thing clear to me. If it's in the Bible, then it's doable! During my Sabbatical, He began to teach me what real rest was. It's more than just ceasing all work and activities; it's a time of reflection and deep meditation. It's saying *no* to myself and *yes* to God. Rest freed me from the chains that kept me bound to the very things I was meant to enjoy as His blessings, not as bondage.

I had fallen prey to the notion that being busy leads to being better, more productive, and accomplishing more. I was addicted to work and found myself tired all the time, drained and easily frustrated. I had no breathing room and I had no margin for error, but all that began to change as God began to renew my mind. The Holy Spirit convicted my heart with the knowledge that overwork meant my faith was lagging. I needed to trust and believe that not only is a weekly Sabbath good for me, but it's also necessary in order for me to enjoy and embrace everything He has called me to do in ministry.

Double Portion

Rather than increase my workload, taking a Sabbath increased my blessings. In this time of ceasing, I discovered the miracle of provision. How could I have forgotten that God is generous in every area? He blesses our obedience and sustains us by graciously giving us twice the harvest without us having to work overtime to get it!

When the Israelites were out in the wilderness, (Exodus 16) Moses instructed them to gather their manna for the day, each family according to their need, and to leave nothing for the following morning lest it become fouled. On the sixth day, he instructed them to pick up twice as much—half for that day and the rest for the following. When asked why this time was different, Moses explained that God was providing for that day and the Sabbath. They didn't have to work more to get the additional manna, it was given to them by God. Why? Because the seventh day is a day of rest, so God provided what was needed for that day, too. It's an unfamiliar principle that says if you work less, you produce more; and, as Christians, we need to remember that God is our provider, not how much or how hard we work. Throughout the Bible we are given many examples of how God loves to multiply. He multiplied twenty loaves of bread and a flask of olive oil in the Second Book of Kings, and five loaves and two fish to feed five thousand hungry people at The Sermon On The Mount in the Gospel of Matthew. God is capable of multiplying and providing us whatever we need, even when it seems impossible. He alone is enough.

This revelation excited me, transforming my heart and mind. By the end of my Sabbatical, my back was back in alignment. More importantly, my soul was again aligned with the truth of God's Word. I discovered a new freedom in my life by placing margins in my week, time to rest and rejuvenate with God. My Sabbatical became the catalyst for a new rhythm and lifestyle where I experienced a double portion of love, grace, peace, tranquility, rest, and even energy.

Some of us are running on fumes. We live day-to-day, barely making it and wondering: *is this all there is to my life?* Life can become monotonous and scary when you are caught on that hamster wheel. This is where the enemy wants to keep you, believing and living this lie. The thief comes to steal, kill, and destroy, but Jesus came so that we could have abundant life. (John 10:10) Your circumstances may not allow you to take an extended Sabbatical, but your circumstances do require you to rest and honor the Sabbath. **Resist the urge to get in the way of what God wants to show you and trust that He wants to multiply some things in your life.**

Are you tired of being tired? You might just need an alignment—a Sabbath from yourself to create an intimacy with God.

Questions for Reflection

1. Do you see any evidence in your life that would suggest people, places, or things have more control in your life than you want to admit? How so?

2. To experience Sabbath in your life, you must make a decision to stop doing something or take a rest from it. What are some things that you need to say no to?

3. If you know that your spiritual life is out of alignment, what are some things you can do to align it with God's heart? What will you need to do to maintain this alignment?

4. Can you recall a time that you said no to someone or something and you experienced a double portion of God's blessing and grace?

Joy

You will fill me with joy in Your presence.
Psalm 16:11

--Pastor Lena

I was new to San Diego and had moved cross-country at a time in my life when I desired to learn more from God. I had met a preacher who visited our Florida church. He had an incredible wealth of knowledge of the Bible and shared truths I had never heard before. He was a scholar, had read the Bible in different languages, and had worked as a consultant for many foreign language translation publishers. I heard this pastor had a church in California and knew I had to be there.

As a single girl in a new town, everything was an exciting adventure. I didn't know what to expect, but I knew whatever God had for me there was going to be life-changing. My first time in the church felt surreal.

Everyone was smiling, everyone seemed happy, and everyone seemed to like each other. Most churches in America have a variety of personalities—depressed members, gossipy members, needy members—the church often looks like a dysfunctional family. But in San Diego, everyone was genuine in their happiness, not just putting on an act for the new girl.

New Friends and New Lessons

As I met people and made new friends, I discovered that their joy was real. My new friend Bridget invited me over to her house, which was about ten minutes away from mine but in a different neighborhood. She had two boys and one girl, and even though she was only a couple years older than me she still seemed so young to have a family. I knew Southern California was an expensive place to live and was surprised to discover she stayed at home with the kids while her husband worked as a handyman. Money was tight for the family. They didn't live extravagantly—they had a modest two-bedroom home and rarely indulged in luxuries like family vacations or big gifts at Christmas. The couple was resourceful with what they had. People in the church gave them clothes, toys, and food for the kids. **God provided for this family, and in return Bridget and her family stayed faithful to Him.**

From Bridget, I learned to be content with what I had. I imagined living a life similar to Bridget's. I knew I would be constantly anxious about my limited finances and the high cost of living in Southern California. Despite all of that, Bridget always had a smile and was joyful. Bridget maintained her joy, no matter what life threw her way, because she found her happiness in God and His love.

Another woman in the church, Tessa, was a mother of three daughters and one boy. I never met her husband, but I heard about him. They co-owned a manufacturing company that was doing very well. The pastor would often pray for her marriage, which I felt meant something was going on. I later learned that rumors were going around town that her husband was possibly having an affair. Tessa did not confront him on the rumors, she trusted God to sort out the situation. Their family was already under tremendous pressure because one of their children was seriously ill. Tessa had every reason to be sad and depressed, but she lived a life genuinely full of joy. I never, not for one second, saw her drop her smile.

I was amazed at how each family I encountered in that church possessed an inner joy that could not be quelled by life's circumstances. I've never seen so many joyful people in one place.

The pastor's wife, Elizabeth, shared with us a story about the day she vowed to live a life full of joy. The church she and her husband started was only a few years old. They were struggling financially while trying to keep up with the rising cost of living in Southern California with two young sons. She managed the family's finances well enough that they always had what they needed, but they also had to count certain things like milk and cheese as a luxury. She recalled going to the grocery store already slightly overwhelmed with managing two boys under the age of five while trying to stick to a grocery list and tight budget. That day, she had just enough money to buy milk. As soon as she got into the house, the family dog ran by her, and so did the two boys. In the chaos, she dropped the bag and spilled the milk.

Elizabeth fell to her knees and started crying. Her husband, sitting a few feet away studying, looked over and said, "What are you doing? There's no sense in crying over spilled milk." She realized at that moment that he was right, it was just milk. In the grand scheme of things, this moment was nothing compared to living a life full of Jesus. **Elizabeth realized that joy should be constant in her life no matter what was happening around her.**

The Gift of Joy

During the months I spent there, I learned one of the essential foundations of our Christian faith—joy is a gift given to us by God and it is not an emotion or a result of conditions around us. Joy is already inside us, and it's up to us to embrace it.

Our acceptance of God's forgiveness through Jesus warrants us forgiveness as well as peace, righteousness, and joy. (Romans 14:17) Reading a little further into

Romans, in Chapter 5, verses 1-5, we see that joy is a freely given gift from God. We need to embrace it, be open to it, and put it to use. How ridiculous would it be to put up your Christmas tree every year, adding the decorations and the presents under the tree, but then never open the gifts? Or you take those wrapped presents and put them in a box, then shelve them along with the tree. Many followers of Jesus take the gifts He's already given us and never open them. We put that joy He has given us away in our closets year after year, never bothering to open the box.

It's one thing to say we need to accept the gift of joy, and it's another to actually figure out *how* to do that. The fastest and easiest way to discover joy is by spending time in God's presence, whether that is through church, prayer, or song. We see many references that correlate between joy and singing or making noise toward God in praise. (Psalm 47:1, Psalm 27:6) In God's presence, there is a fullness of joy. (Psalm 16:11) **Spending time in God's presence can be as simple as reading the Bible or turning on a worship song and singing alon**g. Speaking out loud to God is one great way to spend time in His presence. Sometimes when I'm driving down the road, I start shouting, "Thank you God for this car, for the gas in the tank, for the job I'm driving to, and for paved roads to get me there." He wants to hear us, so speak up and make some noise.

Once you spend time in His presence, you will discover the joy waiting for you. *"Now to Him who is able to keep you from stumbling and to present you blameless before the presence of His glory with great joy, to the only God, our Savior, through Jesus Christ our Lord, be glory, majesty, dominion, and authority, before all time and now and forever. Amen."* (Jude 1:24-25) Time in God's presence will lead to confidence in the gift of joy as this verse says, *"I pray that God, the source of hope, will fill you completely with joy and peace because you trust in him. Then you will overflow with confident hope through the power of the Holy Spirit."* (Romans 15:13 NLT)

When we first recognize that joy is already available to us and we start to spend time in God's presence, the overwhelming confidence in that feeling will overrule any of our negative thoughts. We must continually renew our mind to God's word and renew our mind to what our heart has discovered, so that no matter what happens, we can re-center ourselves in joy. Trials and challenges will come into our lives but they will not overtake our hearts or minds if we stay fixed on being positive. **We have the choice to pick up the gift of joy, especially when life gets hard. (James 1:2-3)** In Philippians 4:4 it says, *"Rejoice in the Lord always. I will say it again: Rejoice!"* The writer is telling the people not once but twice to rejoice and to always have joy in the Lord.

Yes, difficulties will come but go back to His well, and you will weather the storms with strength. I know what you're thinking "You mean still shout for joy, even when a divorce happens, I'm broke, my kids hate me, or my job is laying off people? Shout for joy?" Yes, Joy. King David did when things were not going well for him, *"Then my head will be exalted above the enemies who surround me; at his sacred tent I will sacrifice with shouts of joy; I will sing and make music to the Lord."* (Psalm 27:6)

Expressing joy may be a sacrifice in those difficult moments because you don't feel like making a noise, shouting, or singing, but God is saying to do it anyway. This overflowing joy that is available to you is the key to overcoming the anxiety and stress of any situation. Remember, in His presence is where joy is made confident in you.

Questions for Reflection

1. Can you think of a time when you had overwhelming joy in your life? What was happening?

2. Have you ever experienced complete peace and joy for an extended period?

3. Do you think you can tell the difference between joy and happiness?

4. Read Romans 5:1-11 and James 1:2-4. What good things can come out of the trials and tribulations we endure?

5. Read Psalm 47:1-9, Psalm 27:4-6 & Psalm 16:11. King David shows us a clear way to praise God in difficult times and still have joy. Create your own top three go-to praise and worship songs that you can play and sing along to when things get tough.

6. Read Philippians 4:1-4. Why does the writer tell us to rejoice? (Hint: verse 3)

Loss

*The Lord is close to the brokenhearted
and saves those who are crushed in spirit.*

Psalm 34:18

—Pastor Lucy

My father was dying.

It wasn't a nice, easy death. It was a painful, lingering death brought on by liver cancer. Although I knew it was not realistic, in my mind I kept thinking my dad was going to live forever here on earth. He and my mom were going to be retired and live happily ever after. My father was a staple and a rock, not just in my life, but for all my family as well. Even though his health had been deteriorating for some time, his death was still a shock. A shock because God chose not to heal a perfectly good man, father, husband, brother, and neighbor. At church, we were just finishing up a message series on audacious faith so I knew the enormous power in the prayers that were invading the gates of heaven.

Everyone experiences loss at some point in life. It's inevitable. We lose friends, we lose loved ones; we even lose pets that were loving companions. When someone that you deeply loved dies, it can feel like a part of you has died as well. It's natural to feel sorrow and grief, even when you know they're in a much better place. **Knowing their new eternal home may bring some comfort, but it does not negate feeling a loss of purpose or even emptiness inside.**

In my role as a pastor's wife, I've ministered to many individuals and families who have dealt with a tragedy, whether it be a life-threatening illness or a sudden death. I have been to memorial services, funerals, and supported other families during their time of grief. It's not my favorite place to be, but God tells us in Galatians 6:2: "Carry each other's burdens, and in this way you will fulfill the law of Christ." Although I had spoken words of comfort a hundred times, when my father died in 2012 I realized that death is quite a different experience when you are the one grieving and making the funeral arrangements. In my mind, as much as I wanted to deny my father was dying, eventually my emotions caught up with the reality that no one is promised tomorrow, not even my Papi. It was the moment when my hurt and the Healer collided that God took back His rightful place in my broken heart.

When It Happens to You

Jessica's husband complained of stomach pain when they were on vacation. When it didn't go away, he went to the doctor. And just like that, a young married father of two girls was diagnosed with Stage-4 stomach cancer.

This family had joined our church a few years back and became actively involved by serving on a weekly basis. Joseph dedicated his time in our sound and media department and Jessica served in our children's department. They had two beautiful daughters, one elementary age and the other a teenager. Before the diagnosis, their life was normal. They went to church, work and school. They sat in traffic, cooked dinner, argued and made up. And then their lives turned upside down. Joseph underwent treatments and hospital stays and all of us were hopeful because surely God would heal him and this would make a great miracle story and testimony. **God has done it before, so He could do it again.** Except, for this family (like mine), in just a few short months Joseph was gone and their lives would never be the same.

We don't always understand why God allows certain things to happen in life. We do know that His Word teaches us that His Ways are higher than our ways and His thoughts are higher than our thoughts. (Isaiah 55:8-9) Within a few months after Joseph's passing, all of us who knew the family began to see a miracle unfold in the extraordinary resiliency and capacity of his dear wife. She responded with supernatural grace to this completely unpredictable loss and leaned on God, family, and friends for support. I have seen others in the same situation withdraw and disconnect, remaining stuck in their grief and pain. Jessica pushed through it and let us witness her journey. It didn't happen overnight, and her journey wasn't without bumps and setbacks. It was a process that beautifully unfolded to where God was trying to take Jessica.

Find Strength in Numbers

One of the turning points for Jessica came when she was sitting in a church service. The message asked the question, "How do we face our fears and failures? We do not face them alone. We face them *together*." She realized she had been secretly struggling to keep it together and had been grieving alone. There were others around her who had been impacted by her husband's death, others who loved her and wanted to support her—if only she reached out. On that pew in church, she realized she had to make a conscious decision to either ask for help or be taken under by her grief. Jessica's family was suffering. Her girls were struggling and Jessica was having trouble keeping up in graduate school while juggling the demands of motherhood. She felt incredibly lost. When she finally allowed herself to grieve with her friends and family, the overwhelming sense of support allowed her to feel strong enough to stop hiding and to be transparent. That created even more understanding and support.

There are situations in life that we cannot change or fix but we can overcome them easier when loved ones join us. Jessica's strength came through the community. **When she handed her loss and grief over to God, she began living again.**

Because of that moment in church and her decision to change, Jessica didn't get stuck permanently in her grief or her past because she consciously moved from one season to the next. In our brokenness it is sometimes difficult to see any glimmer of hope or happiness. We long for the normalcy that we knew, even if it wasn't the best situation, yet these familiar words in Scripture tell us otherwise:

> *"For everything there is a season, and a time for every matter under heaven . . ."*
>
> *"A time to weep, and a time to laugh; a time to mourn, and a time to dance . . .."*
>
> —Ecclesiastes 3:1,4

These words invite us to reflect on our current realities. They remind us after every ending there is a beginning of something new, maybe even something better. These common human experiences move us, if we allow ourselves to be moved, from one period of time to another and to experience different emotions, feelings, and thoughts. It doesn't matter if the situation arises from our own free will or whether we were thrust into it with no time to prepare. **God has a plan, and by yielding to His path we can emerge stronger and better.**

His constant faithfulness and steadfast mercy and love are the only things we can trust as we move from one season to the next. He is the only medicine to remedy a broken heart. He is the only one who can help us find hope and peace again, and to bring us back to the life He wants us to lead. **After all, He is the one writing all our stories.**

A year after her husband's death, Jessica finished her master's degree in nursing. Today, she takes each day in stride and has built a strong bond with her daughters. She goes about her days, oblivious to the inspiration she has become for so many. Her end was a new beginning for her, for her children, and for those who know and love her. I know it's not the way she would have written it, but because of this tragic loss she's found a new security and strength she never realized she had. Miracles really do come in all shapes and sizes.

Believe in God; believe in His plan whenever you experience a loss. Trust in Him and take His hand—He is there to help you through it, and to surround you with the people you need to move through that loss and emerge into the future He has planned for you.

Questions for Reflection

1. How did you react to a loss in your life?

2. Have you experienced grief over something other than death?

3. Read Psalm 91:1. What do you gain when you are in the shelter of the Lord? How is that a gain?

4. When bad things happen, do you question God's love for you? What do you do with those feelings?

Self-Reliance

"Blessed is the man who trusts in the Lord, whose trust is the Lord. He is like a tree planted by water, that sends out its roots by the stream, and does not fear when heat comes, for its leaves remain green, and is not anxious in the year of drought, for it does not cease to bear fruit."

Jeremiah 17:7-8

—Pastor Lena

I was at one of my weekly one-on-one sessions with my spiritual mentor, Noelle, when she shared her story with me. She taught me how important it is to rely on God and not on ourselves in times of need. Noelle was the wife of a pastor and explained she'd never imagined she would ever marry, let alone enter a life of ministry, because she nearly lost her life to alcoholism.

Noelle grew up with alcoholic parents who divorced when she was five. She had always wanted to stay single, to save herself the heartache of divorce. She dreamed of being a lawyer and of serving justice after she graduated college. All was almost lost when she started down the same path to alcoholism as her parents.

A friend recognized her need for help, told her about Jesus, and invited her to church. A month later, that spiritual connection inspired Noelle to change her life. She set about finishing college and preparing to take the LSAT so she could enter law school. Her professors wrote glowing recommendations about her college accomplishments: leading a protest against unfair wages for women, tutoring low income kids in an after-school program, maintaining a high GPA, and working part-time as a secretary.

It's Not All You

Noelle, however, had endured a life filled with disappointment; and even though she loved her church, she had yet to learn to rely on God. She went through so much as a child that she did not want to leave herself vulnerable to anyone. She wanted to be wholly self-reliant, both financially and emotionally. So she opted to live alone in her senior year and vowed to be completely independent.

About a month before graduation, a traveling female preacher came to Noelle's church as a guest minister.

It was during that church service God revealed to Noelle that she was, indeed, living in total self-reliance. Noelle had created a life where she did not need anyone to help accomplish her goals, not even God. She had created systems in her life that would protect her if something went wrong. For instance, if her professors refused to write recommendations, she could apply without them and market herself to get accepted. Rather than rely on a roommate to split the rent, she lived modestly in a studio apartment she could afford on her own. God showed her that living alone closed the opportunity for Noelle to develop any strong female friendships. Yet she did not make any major life changes after leaving that church service. **She heard the message but didn't take it to heart.** She continued with her plans for law school. Noelle continued to live life alone, and she continued to set and meet goals.

During Noelle's second year in law school, the same woman returned to her church, and something incredible happened. The minister said she wanted to pray for Noelle. "God spoke to you a year ago about changing something in your heart," the minister said, "and you were disobedient and did not let God do His work." Noelle remembered the message she had heard a year earlier and realized she hadn't applied God's message in her life.

After the minister left, Noelle was determined to make the changes she needed, but learning to trust God was not easy. She moved into a different apartment and got a roommate, but God was directing Noelle to do more. A few months later, the minister returned again and spoke at her church. She spotted Noelle in the lobby and, after they exchanged some small talk, she asked Noelle if she would be interested in traveling with her as an assistant.

Noelle was stunned. She had only talked to this woman once before and now she felt like God was sending her in a whole new direction. As she shared this story, Noelle explained to me that when God teaches someone a lesson, He will eventually test them to be sure they have learned it. Here was her test, but what a life-changing decision it would be.

Noelle heard God's message and decided to give up the life she had built to travel the world with someone she hardly knew, trusting God would take care of everything she needed. She figured she could travel with the minister for a year and if it didn't work out, she would just return to school. **You see, Noelle still had a backup plan; deep down inside, she was still struggling to trust God.**

By saying yes to the minister, Noelle had taken a big step in her Christian walk toward truly trusting God with her life. She also chose to trust the minister, who became her mentor. That fall, they traveled throughout Europe, and that winter they visited a church in Oklahoma. The pastor of this church was a young, single man who had just been put in charge of the church a year earlier.

He and Noelle developed a friendship, then exchanged numbers and kept in touch after she left. Noelle fell in love with him and moved to Oklahoma to see him more. The two started getting into arguments over petty things. To escape conflict, Noelle would threaten to leave the relationship and live her life alone. Her threats to leave and her continual avoidance of their issues hurt their relationship deeply. Noelle was terrified because she didn't want to end up with the same heartache her divorced parents had suffered, but it seemed inevitable.

When the traveling minister came back to town for a visit, Noelle told her the relationship was falling apart. Noelle was done and wanted to go back to law school.

The minister asked one simple question: *Are you trusting God as much as you can?*

In that moment, everything changed for Noelle. She'd forgotten to trust God and retreated into old patterns of being alone and self-reliant. In doing so, she was pushing away the man who loved her. She could either choose to trust God, who had put this man in her life, or rely entirely on herself.

I looked down that day at the wedding ring on her finger and the smile on her face and knew she had made the right choice, the one that God wanted her to make, and God had provided her with a wonderful life.

It's Not a Sin, but a Roadblock

In the last few decades, society has told women they should strive to be independent from others, including God. It's okay to have some self-reliance—ensuring you have a job and an income, and to set and maintain goals. **However, sometimes people rely on themselves so much it gets in the way of trusting God.** *"Not that we are sufficient in ourselves to claim anything as coming from us, but our sufficiency is from God."* (2 Corinthians 3:5) By not trusting in God, we paralyze the working power of God in our lives. God has an abundant life available to us for which we do not need to strive, so we do not have to rely on our own strength to accomplish anything. He has made it clear we are to find our strength in life in God, *"I can do all things through him who strengthens me."* (Philippians 4:13)

Noelle initially wanted to live relying on herself and her accomplishments, which the Bible warns against, *"For by the grace given me I say to every one of you: Do not think of yourself more highly than you ought, but rather think of yourself with sober judgment, in accordance with the faith God has distributed to each of you."* (Romans 12:3) The danger of living a life of self-reliance is that it can easily cross over into pride. Noelle developed an attitude of pride regarding her accomplishments. (Proverbs 8:13)

It was that pride that kept her from changing when God spoke to her the first time. Pride told her, 'I hear what God said but I don't need to change.' **Pride makes its own plans in life, without asking for direction from God.** Pride will say 'I have done all these things, my talent, my gifts, my abilities, my intelligence, it's all done because of the work *I* have done.' The attitude of pride causes self-righteous behavior, which is clearly taught in 1 Corinthians. The Apostle Paul told the church in Corinth that they were not responsible for all the money and gifts they received. Rather, it was God's grace on the people that was the reason why they received such a blessing.

Noelle's pride raged when she entered that dating relationship. Pride will reveal itself when put to the test. She was being pressed in the relationship to make a commitment, which made her true prideful self-emerge, exposing all the hidden things she had not yet dealt with. When pride is exposed, what follows is its destruction. (Proverbs 16:18) This is what happened to Noelle. Her pride led her to a place where she risked losing that relationship because she was pushing people away, just to maintain her self-sufficiency. She grew comfortable in herself, and thought there was no need for anyone else. God was working to remove that pride, to show her that He was all she needed.

If you find yourself living a life of pride, you must ask God for forgiveness and then surrender your life to Him. Ask God to show you where you have eliminated Him from your life and then humble yourself daily in that area. "*But seek first the kingdom of God and His righteousness, and all these things will be given to you as well."* (Matthew 6:33) A life in total surrender to God is the most freeing way to live. Noelle wanted me to learn that lesson during our mentorship meeting because she wanted me to apply it in my own marriage and life. Her example has served as a lesson in allowing God to remove the roadblocks of self-reliance so that we can more freely travel the path He wishes us to walk.

God has an abundant life available for us—all we need to do is lean on Him. *"I can do all things through Him who strengthens me."* (Philippians 4:13)

Questions for Reflection

1. If you were to list your accomplishments like a resumé, what would it sound like?

2. How many of your accomplishments did you achieve by yourself? How many did you accomplish with the help of others or a team of people?

3. Do you think you are living a life of self-reliance or God-reliance?

4. Read 2 Corinthians 3:4-6. Has God made us self-sufficient or reliant on Him to accomplish goals?

5. Read Romans 12:1-5. Why doesn't the writer want you to be prideful?

6. Read Proverbs 16:18-20. What is the result of being humble and trusting God?

Acceptance

*"I praise you because I am fearfully
and wonderfully made;
Your works are wonderful, I know
that full well."*

Psalm 139:14

—Pastor Lucy

Every second of the day, someone is being judged for their looks, their words, or their thoughts. Our private selves have become public and the people in our circle (even strangers) are finding it acceptable to comment, bully, or ridicule us. Teenagers, especially girls, face this pressure as social media becomes more of the norm and the veil of the internet allows people to say things they might not say to someone's face.

The by-product of all this judgment is a negative self-image. Girls feel pressured, both by peers and by themselves, to be accepted and "liked" on social media. They may perpetuate an image as a party girl or a fighter, just to align their social image with pop culture. As a consequence, many young girls today are growing up with an unhealthy view of themselves, measuring their self-worth by what people post about them. **Their focus is on the secular world, not on God's world.**

This creates a paradox that many young people don't even realize is happening in their hearts and minds: *The more you try to live your life in accordance to God's Word, then the less accepted you will feel.* By distancing yourself from God, who loves you just as you are, you miss out on the richest acceptance of all and end up living your life constantly chasing an ever-elusive social status.

Teenagers between the ages of twelve and seventeen report using text messages in their daily lives more than any other form of communication, including face-to-face interaction (Lenhart, 2010). Their text communication includes emoji, chat acronyms, and slang—shortened communication that doesn't utilize the language and nuances of interpersonal contact or even letters. Teens today have more technology and resources at their fingertips than every previous generation, yet experts say today's kids are growing up with more anxiety and less self-esteem than ever before. There are a high percentage of teenagers suffering from depression and identity crises. As a result, the pressure keeps mounting for them, especially when they are being bombarded with so many different images and messages from media, music, culture, magazines, peers, and us—the adults in their lives.

Pressure and Trust

Part and parcel with finding acceptance is dealing with peer pressure and finding people whose opinions and guidance you can trust. I recently spoke to two sisters, sixteen-year-old Demi and fourteen-year-old Jada. Demi plays percussion in the marching band at her school while Jada enjoys playing basketball. Both are normal teenage girls who face the same challenges almost every girl faces today, but they deal with them in different ways.

Demi feels constant pressure to keep everyone happy, including herself. Then there is the pressure to determine what she wants to be or do upon graduating from high school, pressure to keep her GPA up to continue playing in band, and pressure to get accepted into college. Every day of her life is part of this pressure cooker to perform well in order to avoid disappointing her family, friends, and especially herself. For Demi, making everyone happy is part of how she feels accepted.

Jada has dealt with the fallout from broken trust. Like many teenage girls looking for acceptance among her peers, she rushed into friendships and caved to peer pressure on social media—two choices that resulted in cyberbullying. Since then, her challenge has been finding true friends she can trust, who accept her for who she is.

Both girls saw the impact of social media on their self-acceptance. However, not all teenagers are quick to limit their use of Snapchat, Instagram, etc. For them, the negativity, bullying, and put-downs have driven the sisters to use their time in other ways. They have added more extra-curricular activities into their schedules, to find more positive outlets and places to make friends.

As adults, how many of us feel the same way as these teenagers did? Do we still worry about how other people see us, whether we are meeting their expectations, and whether we can trust our circle to not only accept us but to love us just as we are?

Demi and Jada have learned to be comfortable in their own skin, even when others don't accept them. The girls' perspective on life and their faith in God gave them this self-assurance. They have seen the impact of peer pressure on others and the way other girls in their circle have lied, cheated, bullied, etc., just to be accepted. Those experiences taught them that the opinions of their peers should not influence how they feel about themselves.

These two young girls believe that they have been fearfully and wonderfully made (Psalm 139:14), something that not even many adult believers can grasp, understand, or believe. For them, it meant that not everyone is supposed to look, talk, or act the same. We are different, but God loves us just the way we are because He made us. What a great revelation to know and experience at such a young age.

> *"The first step toward change is awareness.
> The second step is acceptance."*
>
> – Writer and psychotherapist, Nathaniel Branden

Teaching Ourselves and the Next Generation

Adults face these same issues. So many of us compare ourselves to others based on the perceptions we have of those around us, due in no small part to social media. Keep in mind, it is a *perception*, not a reality. That friend with the perfect husband or model children is very likely only presenting one view of her life. We need to stop comparing our weights, our homes, and our lives to those around us and accept ourselves just as we are—just as God made us to be.

We also need to model that acceptance to younger generations. These sisters are a prime example of why it is so important for us to teach and train our younger generation just like the writer Paul admonishes in Titus 2. It is a task for older women to train younger women how to live a Christian life in their relationships, living wisely, and making a life of following God appealing to other believers.

Demi and Jada are accepting what their parents have taught them and what God's Word says. Both of these girls are headed for greatness and have the potential to change the world because of everything they are learning at such a young, pivotal age. But there are many more like them who haven't been told they are valuable, loved, and accepted by their Creator. Instead, they are looking for love, worth, and acceptance in all the wrong places. Should they continue down this wrong path, it will only lead to rejection and pain.

Everyone wants to be accepted and to fit in with their social circle, but isn't it far more important to fit in with God's view and His love? **Christ sees us at our best and at our worst, yet He completely accepts us just the way we are.** Instead of magazine covers telling us we need thinner thighs or smoother skin, imagine the following headlines: *"You are worth fighting for!" The Lord will fight for you.* (Exodus 14:14) *You are chosen.* (Ephesians 1:4) *You are loved just the way you are!"* (Jeremiah 31:3) Through reading and accepting phrases like these might very well change the perspectives we have of ourselves, others, and God.

Social media can be a powerful tool used to change lives for better or for worse. However, we can use social media and the power of our voices to be the catalyst that brings change to other women and girls. Acceptance is so much more than clicking the "like" button or a comment on a social media post. **Acceptance is strength in the knowledge that God loves every detail about yourself—the good, the bad, the ugly, and all the in-between, and then smiling because He's okay with that.** It's about loving yourself as God loves you. Be a model of that love and start today. Empowered women empower women.

> *If you live for people's acceptance,*
> *you will die from their rejection.*
>
> – Hip hop artist, LeCrae

Questions for Reflection

1. Do you ever worry about what other people think about you? Why or why not?

2. How did you handle wanting to be accepted as a teenager? What challenges were different for you?

3. In what ways do you think you can make a difference in the life of a teen girl?

4. Colossians 2:10 says you are complete in God's eyes. How does this change your perspective about yourself? How about your perspective of the next generation?

Success

*The Lord was with Joseph,
and he was a successful man....*

Genesis 39:2

—Pastor Lena

Success.

So many of us define that word by what we accomplish at work, how far we advance in our careers, or what awards sit on our shelves. We think, *if I can just [whatever goal you set] then I'll feel and look successful.*

I was the same way. I worked in an industry where success and career advancement was based on what you brought to the table each day. One Monday morning, I was sitting in a pitch meeting for a local television station. I was one of the producers, and it was my job to listen to the reporters' ideas and pick the best one, the story that would be the lead on the evening news. I sat there with the other producers, listening to variations on the same pitches as always: A story about the debate over trash pickup. A scoop about a famous director who was in town scouting a film location. A follow-up on a shooting that happened over the weekend.

Instead of focusing on the reporters around me, I found myself daydreaming about that weekend. I'd spent time with two teenage girls I was mentoring, one who was dealing with insecurity issues and another with a gravely ill mother. I saw my friends, all in their early twenties, on Saturday night and heard them say they thought I was a "success" because I was finished with school and just landed the "perfect job" with a decent salary. Sunday, after church, I worked with a youth ministry. It was the biggest one in the city, with around eight hundred students. It had been a busy but emotionally satisfying weekend and I found myself looking forward to doing more work with the kids the following weekend.

"Lena, which story do you like for your lead?" my news director asked me, dragging me out of my thoughts.

I answered, "I guess I'll go with the shooting."

Because my newscast was the top-rated newscast in the city and was number one in the nation for its time slot, I was given first pick in the pitch sessions. To my friends and coworkers, it seemed as though I had hit the jackpot following graduation. Great references, an amazing job on a top newscast, and a healthy salary. **It seemed that God's blessing was on my life!**

Still, I felt a growing unrest. As I sat at my desk later, making more decisions and writing the news copy, I couldn't help but think back to how I had spent my weekend. Instead of feeling fulfilled and feeling God's blessing in my job at the television station, it felt like I was going to be wasting the next seven hours of my workday. I started to think my weekend had been more of a success than this next newscast would ever be. *What am I doing with my life?* I thought.

How much more meaningful was that conversation with thirteen-year old Tiffany about her self-worth? She was entering high school and starting to navigate the dynamics of friendships, deciding which ones had value to her self-identity. Did God hear my prayer when I prayed with fourteen-year old Lauren about her mom's cancer? Lauren's mother was facing a recurrence of her breast cancer. And with her dad out of her life, Lauren feared one day she would be left an orphan. How much more intentional were those conversations than the daily newsroom conversation about crimes or film producers in this city?

Suddenly, it hit me like a ton of bricks: **God had changed my definition of success.** He was moving me into a season of ministry, a time that I would have to set aside my current career to focus on Him and learn how to teach others about Jesus. God was changing the course of my life right before my eyes. I felt a tug to go back to school with a focus on ministry. When I said "Yes" to this course change in my life, God laid out the plan, step-by-step. He provided the money and the place to live, and I answered His call.

What Is Success?

From the beginning of our lives, the secular world gives us different definitions of success. Some say it's a certain financial status or a certain type of home, and others a family that looks a certain way.

Success in God's eyes is completely opposite to the world's definition of success. With God, we see success in the lives of people in the Bible who acted in simple obedience to God. God wants our lives to be in complete obedience to both His known and unknown will for our lives. God's known will is what we see written in the Bible. **Through the Ten Commandments, God has given us the blueprint for how to be obedient in our lives.**

Learning God's unknown will for your life requires getting close to Him and listening for His words. God may speak directly to your heart, He may give you a dream in the night, a vision you see like a daydream, or an audible voice. God's unknown will for our lives are those specific details that are just for us, like if we should marry a certain person, what career to pursue, or what business decisions to make. These answers aren't found in the Bible. They're in the words God speaks to us.

By being obedient to and drawing close to God, we find the success we've been searching for. The Bible is filled with stories about people who did this. Joseph, for example, was sold into slavery by his own brothers, then imprisoned, and falsely accused. Through it all, he remained a dreamer and a visionary. *"The Lord was with Joseph,"* (Genesis 39:2) shows that Joseph's relationship with God was special, but also one we can all have, if we draw close to Him. Because God was close to Joseph, Genesis Chapter 39 goes on to say, *"he was a successful man."* A man with nothing is a success? Seems contradictory to what a business leader would say.

Redefine "Success" for You

My definition of success changed when I drew closer to God. Before and during college my relationship with Jesus was like the kind you might have with an acquaintance. I knew His name and I knew where to find Him if I needed Him. It took active work on my part to become intimate with Jesus and make him one of the best friends in my life, and what a difference that made! When we draw close and spend time with Him we are better able to figure out who we really are and what's important in our lives.

When I had that 'aha moment' at work, God was able to show me my heart's hidden desire—to help children discover Jesus for themselves. My act of obedience first began in drawing near to God, discovering His will and then acting on it. I could have decided not to follow God's instruction to pursue graduate school. I could have stayed in my "dream job," and had the world's version of success, but that would mean I was making my own choices and going against what God already instructed me to do.

Throughout the Bible, there are many examples of God instructing the people who have drawn close to Him. Noah is a good example. Instructed to build an ark, he was mocked for his obedience but he still obeyed. By following God's instructions, he was able to save himself, his family, as well as a multitude of animals from the flood. Noah's obedience paid off and led to him becoming an heir of righteousness. (Hebrews 11:7)

Our obedience to God is the only measure of success we should live by. It is His approval and standard of living we should strive to abide by. We will only learn how to be obedient by first reading His Word, then by drawing close to Him, and being obedient to His instructions.

Overall, it is important to realize that true success comes from our obedience to what God reveals to us when we draw close to Him. In that, you will find satisfaction and joy.

Questions for Reflection

1. How do you define success?

2. What would God consider a success in your own life?

3. What is your plan to draw closer to God?

4. How does God tell you His unknown will for your own life? Dream? Vision? Voice? Heart Tug?

5. Read Mark 12:41-44. There is no indicator of the amount of time the widow spent drawing close to God in order to build up her faith to the point where she gave everything she had. Do you believe you have enough faith to give up something of great value if God asked? Can you think of a time you showed great obedience to God, like the widow?

6. Read Hebrews 11:1-40. Several examples are given of people displaying great faith which leads to an obedient heart to do God's will. Pick one of the examples given and think of what would have happened if that person had NOT been obedient to God's instruction. Would the outcome have been the same? What consequences would have happened had that person been disobedient?

Control

"For my thoughts are not your thoughts, neither are your ways my ways, declares the Lord. As the heavens are higher than the earth, so are my ways higher than your ways and my thoughts than your thoughts."

Isaiah 55:8-9

—Pastor Lucy

Imagine the scene: Jesus and His disciples were on route to Jerusalem but He decided to make a stop at Martha's house since it was on the way. There was excitement and anticipation in the air, but there was also hustle and commotion inside of Martha's house as she prepared for the guest of all guests. She's hurrying around, sweeping, doing dishes, making the bed, starting dinner, and yelling out to her sister Mary for help with the chores.

When Jesus finally arrived, the sisters gave Him a warm welcome and invited Him to make himself at home. Martha was the worrywart, so she ran around the house seeing to His needs, while Mary—who perhaps felt indebted to this remarkable friend who had raised her brother, Lazarus, from the dead after three days in the tomb—stands transfixed. There was a special bond that they all shared with Jesus. (John 11:5) Although she couldn't articulate it, I'm sure Mary felt drawn to His gentle eyes and His soothing words. After all, she had done the housework to prepare for His visit; now she just wanted to enjoy their guest. Martha, however, was still worried about the house and the preparations.

The story of Mary and Martha is a popular account recorded in the Bible in Luke 10:38-42. This narrative is one that many women can relate to and can certainly identify with because, at one time or another, we have all been one of these sisters.

Martha believed there was still more work to be done in the kitchen. She felt anxious and irritated that everyone, especially her sister, seemed to be having a good time in the living room while she was alone in the kitchen preparing the food they were all going to eat. She could hear Jesus tell them all about his journey and all the people he had met along the way. Martha was angry and wondered why Jesus hadn't sent Mary to the kitchen to help. Martha walked into the room and complained to Jesus. His response to her is so precious. *"My dear Martha, you are worried and upset over all these details! There is only one thing worth being concerned about. Mary has discovered it, and it will not be taken away from her."* (verses 41-42)

There are so many different lessons that we can obtain from Mary, Martha, and Jesus.

The most important one is in Jesus' response to Martha: *"worried and upset over many things."* Women have a natural tendency to worry, fret, plan, pre-plan, plan again, and run minute details over and over again in their heads. In other words, some—well, maybe most women—like to be in control. Control is power. Control is security. **When you have control over something, you know it's going to get done the way that you planned and if not, someone else is to blame**. People who like to have control often think there is only one right way to do something. They use their power to not only control details but to manage other people's actions and responses. However, maintaining a tight grip of control can have the opposite effect—it can make your life spin out of control because you are constantly scrambling to secure everything and everyone in place.

You're constantly worried about all the details that go not just into today, but tomorrow, next week, and next month, etc. Typically, women who have difficulty managing and expressing their inner feelings have a strong tendency to control their external relationships, work setting, family and/or friends. They can be emotionally unstable and may suffer from depression, anxiety, low self-esteem, lack of trust, abuse, or painful emotions due to trauma. When these emotions are left untreated and unresolved, they can manifest themselves physically through eating disorders, body image issues, self-harm, addictions, etc. Control actually ends up creating a world *out of control*, which is the point Jesus was trying to make.

A False Sense of Security

From a young age, Alexandra enjoyed and needed to be in charge. Although she was the baby sister, she was the one who ordered her sister around. Always the planner, she was the one who stepped up and organized anything that was not in order. For her, security came in knowing a plan was in place and how the day was going to unfold. There was safety in having control and knowing the details beforehand. There was also satisfaction in experiencing the rewards of a well-thought out and executed plan. Anything that breached this controlled structure would wreak havoc in Alexandra's mind and send her into a frenzy. A failed plan brought feelings of insecurity and helplessness. By the time she became a teenager, this need for control manifested itself through an eating disorder, anxiety attacks, and major depression. At the root of these conditions were issues of control, self-esteem, trust, and the inability to cope with the realities of life events. For Alexandra, her eating disorder offered a false sense of control that consequently resulted in a total loss of power over her life. In trying to control so much, her life had spun out of control.

It wasn't until she was in her mid-twenties that she made a conscious decision to trust God and to understand why her life mattered to Him. This decision to relinquish control and give her life to God gave her a new sense of freedom she had never experienced before. With the help of a therapist, she began the process of restoring her life one day at a time, learning to face and embrace all the unknowns in life. In essence, Alexandra began to live in faith that God was the only one in total control. **This liberated her to make mistakes and know she was still loved.** It freed her from the mental worry and stress of trying to control every detail of her life and sometimes that of others. Truly understanding every aspect of who God was released any desire to be in control of every situation. She learned to feel safe in Him and brought people into her life who showed her what genuine love felt like; what real friends looked like.

What Really Matters

Like Mary, Alexandra discovered the one thing worth being concerned about: God's will for us. To do this means that, every day, we choose what we think is the highest priority; which, as the Bible tells us, is to "*seek first His kingdom and His righteousness, and all these things will be given to you as well.*" (Matthew 6:33) Seeking God means depending on Him to unveil His will—His plan and His details for your life, in His timing. **It means ceding control to God, in all ways and in all things.**

Why should we do this? Because He has our best interests at heart (see Jeremiah 29:11). His plans are much better than any we could ever conjure up and His ways are much higher than our ways. Jesus wasn't telling Martha that preparing dinner or doing housework was not important. Jesus was speaking directly to her heart. He saw past her need to perform and saw a heart that was overwhelmed with the details of life. Her outspoken demand was in response to a heart contaminated by fear and pride. In contrast, Mary chose the Words of Jesus and being in his presence as the most important thing for her to do.

Jesus says in John 10:10, "*I have come that they may have life, and have it to the full.*" In order to experience all blessings that God has for you, you have to exchange your life of control for a life of surrender. As we practice a life of surrender we will begin to notice a change in our character that leads to a change in our behavior. It becomes easier to welcome the unexpected in our lives. So, we respond to others with grace instead of as harsh judges when things go awry. Handing over control to God gives you peace and joy. **Giving control to God is bravery at its finest!**

Questions for Reflection

1. In what ways do you relate to Martha? To Mary?

2. What are some areas in your life that you know you have a firm grip on and what areas are difficult for you to let go?

3. What are the things that frustrate you in life and why?

4. How can you demonstrate daily surrender to God?

Anger

*Refrain from anger, and turn from wrath;
do not fret-it leads only to evil.*

Psalm 37:8

—Pastor Lena

Chris and I were on our first date when I realized he had an issue with anger. We spent much of the evening talking about our families and laughing about our experiences that year in Bible college. We talked about funny things we witnessed during class and with our friends. The conversation naturally segued to a moment in class when I saw Chris yelling at one of our former classmates. Chris was screaming at the other student and accusing him of lying. I wasn't sure what happened between them, but it caused so much of a scene that two other students had to step in and separate them.

"What happened that day?" I asked.

Chris told me that the other student accused him of cheating because Chris got an A on a paper. It wasn't true and Chris was very angry about the accusation. I was surprised by how casually Chris talked about that day because I truly thought the altercation would come to blows. He looked me straight in the eye and said, "I wasn't angry. You haven't seen me angry yet."

Then he took a deep breath and started to share his story.

Chris grew up in a very traditional family. His mom and dad were married for over forty years. He had three brothers, two older and one younger. The entire family attended church every Sunday. Chris was sexually abused when he was a toddler. And while he didn't think the abuse contributed to his anger problems, I was well aware that studies regarding the effects of such a horrific event said otherwise.

The first time Chris remembered getting angry was with his older brothers. Because of the age difference, he wasn't as close as the older brothers were. They often excluded him by ignoring him at home and not inviting him to hang out. Chris told me he remembered being so angry that he'd go down to the basement and punch a hole in the wall to release some of his pent-up frustration.

Growing up, he made some of the mistakes as other teenagers and chose the wrong group of friends, people who were a bad influence and who convinced him to steal, lie, use drugs, and commit robbery. At only twelve years old, he had little supervision and was out of control. He was in trouble with the law and in and out of rehab. Chris found himself a dropout in middle school. The drug problem that Chris struggled with only fueled his anger because instead of making him feel calm and relaxed, the drugs would unleash his anger.

At seventeen, Chris was offered one final chance to get his life straight by going to a drug rehab facility. The judge warned Chris that if he violated the terms of his release to rehab that he would go straight to the state prison instead of the juvenile facility. It was only then that Chris realized he had allowed anger to rule his life. He knew the next few months in rehab would be a critical turning point in his life.

In rehab, Chris returned to something he had left a long time ago—prayer. He remembered learning in Sunday school class that the only way he could be healed of anger was by leaning on Jesus. Over and over, he whispered the same simple prayers he had learned as a child, but he still struggled with his faith. One night on his knees, he closed his eyes, bowed his head, and vowed, "Jesus, if I can't feel You, touch You, or hear You like I can do with my brothers, then forget it. That's what I am going to need from You to live this life with You."

In that moment, Chris physically felt someone walk into the room. Overwhelming peace flooded his heart. When he tried to raise his head to see who had walked into the room, he couldn't. He realized it was because Jesus was standing in the room with him. The weight of God's presence was thick, making the air stand still. When he finally got up and went outside, the world seemed brighter, more vibrant, the air in Queens fresh and clean. He cried then, and as he recounted the story to me, tears filled his eyes.

That day, when Jesus walked into his room, was the day Chris let go of his anger, shame, sin, resentment, as well as his drug addiction. From that day forward, he experienced the same frustrations as other people but never the anger that once ruled his life. It took a moment shared with Jesus to take it away. **Anger is not part of God's DNA and shouldn't be part of a human's DNA, either.** When we recognize God's character, it makes it easier to recognize the reality of Jesus in our lives.

The Two Types of Anger

When God first created man and woman, He did not put anger into them. It didn't become part of the Adamic nature until after the fall of man, when sin entered the world. (Genesis 3) Anger makes an appearance in human history quickly after the fall of man in Genesis 4, when Adam and Eve's son Cain kills their other son Abel. Cain killed his brother because he was angry with God and took it out on his brother. Through the story of the first siblings in the Bible, God shows us the consequences of anger.

This story repeats itself in modern history as the same dynamic of anger plays out in families. A husband comes home, upset about something that happened at work, and directs his anger towards his wife and kids, sometimes ending in horrible consequences.

There are two types of anger—unrighteous and righteous anger. Unrighteous anger is a lack of Godly character, meaning a lack of self-control and a lack in the fruit of the spirit. This kind of anger is often rooted in other sins, like lust, envy, jealousy, hate, and resentment. God has a stern warning for his students about unrighteous anger. He says, *"My dear brothers and sisters, take note of this: Everyone should be quick to listen, slow to speak and slow to become angry, because human anger does not produce the righteousness that God desires."* (James 1:19-20) According to God, unrighteous anger leads to a negative response, *"Refrain from anger, and forsake wrath! Fret not yourself; it tends only to evil."* (Psalms 37:8)

God does get angry, but His anger is not rooted in sin. God's anger is at sin and at the products of sin. God's anger is called righteous anger——that's when things, events, or actions, dishonor God and bring suffering. When God feels righteous anger toward His children, the consequences are often dire. *"So the Lord was very angry with Israel and removed them from His presence. Only the tribe of Judah was left."* (2 Kings 17:18) God was willing to wipe out an entire generation of people because of their sin. Righteous anger is produced once the fruits of the spirit, *"love, joy, peace, patience, kindness, goodness, faithfulness, gentleness, and self-control,"* (Galatians 5:22-23), become missing from one's life.

Once a believer has self-control, then righteous anger can be seen in their life. Jesus displayed righteous anger in Mark 3:5: *"He looked around at them in anger and, deeply distressed at their stubborn hearts, said to the man, 'Stretch out your hand.' He stretched it out, and his hand was completely restored."* In Mark 3, Jesus was angry at the blindness in people's hearts that was preventing a healing miracle from happening. Righteous anger directed at a sin or a person committing that sin should provoke change. Righteous anger turns the heart back toward God; it points back at the One who is good and pure. This is why God distinguishes the difference between righteous and unrighteous anger. People who love Jesus and possess the fruit of the spirit have this warning, *"In your anger do not sin. Do not let the sun go down while you are still angry."* (Ephesians 4:26)

If we have unrighteous anger, we must first recognize that the root comes straight from the Devil, who is angry with God. The Devil is working to destroy everything precious to God— which is you and me. In Revelations 12, the Devil came down to earth with great anger towards God's creation. The Devil knows that he can restrain a person in a sinful trap if he can make him or her angry. Sin separates us from God's presence and power in our lives, but it does not separate us from God's love.

To resist the Devil, we must work like farmers who want to grow a strong crop. The farmer prepares the field, plants a seed, watches the crop grow, pulls infiltrating weeds, and chases away animals that try to steal the crop. Once the crop is harvested, the farmer has food. Cultivating the fruit of the spirit works the same way. We must prepare our hearts to receive from God what He wants us to do in our lives.

Our hearts should feast on love, joy, peace, patience, kindness, goodness, faithfulness, gentleness, and self-control. These fruits prevent the heart from falling prey to sin and will stop anger from taking effect. **God wants His people to live a life free of anger, and to live a life free of sin.** This takes time and the surrendering our hearts to God's will. Open yourself to Him, and He will come into the room and be there to fill your soul with peace instead of anger.

Oh, and in case you didn't know, I eventually married Chris. He is the calmest, sweetest man I know, and because he has struggled with his faith and obedience, he is a leader to those around him. When he walks into a room, he brings a sense of calm and love that embraces all who know him.

Questions for Reflection

1. Think of a time in your life you were so angry that you harmed or thought about harming someone else. What did you do?

2. What is your immediate response after you get angry? Do you cry, ask for forgiveness, or take deep breaths?

3. Does someone in your life deal with anger? What do you think is the root cause of that anger?

4. Read Genesis 4:1-15. Why does Cain hate his brother so much? What was God's response to Cain's anger?

5. Read 2 Kings 17:13-21. What was Israel doing that caused God to become so angry?

6. Read Galatians 5:16-26. Make a list of the characteristics of a sinful nature. Make a list of a Godly nature or spiritual fruits. Compare the two lists and see which characteristics you need to remove from your life and which you need to cultivate.

Faith

For you know that when your faith is tested, your endurance has a chance to grow.

James 1:3

—Pastor Lucy

Imagine you are on a ship at sea and a great storm kicks up. Before you can get your sea legs, you are thrown overboard. You're trying hard to swim for shore, or to grab something—anything—to keep yourself from drowning, but before you can . . . you're swallowed by a whale. That would certainly seem like the end, right? Or would it actually be another moment to test your faith?

We don't all have moments like Jonah did in the Bible, but each of us has moments that test our faith. The bank account that is overdrawn just when the mortgage is due, a sick child who is lying in a hospital bed, or even a new job in another country meaning starting all over again. We may be sitting by a dying loved one's bedside, or answering another stressful call, and feel our faith wavering or even disappearing. It happens to all of us at one time or another. Hopefully, like Jonah, it will result in us acknowledging that God is our salvation.

In some churches, they use the phrase, "count it all joy". How is it possible to feel joy when you are in the middle of one of life's trials? This statement is taken from James 1:2, where the author tells readers to count trials and troubles as an opportunity for great joy. Quite an oxymoron, wouldn't you say? Does that mean I should be happy when I get a flat tire, or my child's grades are suffering, or I just got laid off? In context, James isn't saying be happy about the current circumstance, but be joyful about what the outcome will bring. God is up to something. There are some new things He wants us to learn through the current situation. **If we go through trials with an open mind and an open heart, then there will be opportunities for new levels of maturity.** On the other hand, if we approach His trials with the wrong attitude, they will not end until we finally see and understand what God is trying to show us.

James follows that phrase by saying our endurance has a chance to grow when our faith is tested. I don't know about you, but just hearing that exhausts me. I've been through enough unwanted trials and tests in my lifetime that I prefer to avoid them if possible. If I am totally honest about those moments, I admit

I have successfully endured the good and the bad, the highs and the lows, the passing and the failing. God has carried me through every storm, and every storm has eventually yielded to sunshine. It doesn't mean I'll never be tested again. My walk of faith will be a continual "test" until the day that I physically leave this earth. This means that I have to keep practicing my faith in God if I want to pass.

Faith is like a muscle—the more that you exercise it, the stronger it becomes and your endurance increases. When you consistently target specific muscles in your body during workouts, the more powerful those muscles become. They may be really sore in the beginning, you may even be in pain, but eventually they will strengthen and be there to support your body when it is weakened by illness, injury, or exhaustion. Faith is a lot like that. The more you exercise complete trust and confidence in God, the stronger you become in the face of the unpleasant challenges in your life and the more you will know He is there to support you when you are feeling weak.

The Trials of Faith

Any time we venture out into this life of faith, something in our circumstances will always conflict with our belief—that is the moment when our faith is tested. Without this test, however, there would be no need to exercise our faith, and a lack of exercise would result in our faith growing weak. We can prepare for these exercises by remembering what is said in Romans 8:28, *"And we know that in all things God works for the good of those who love Him, who have been called according to His purpose."*

My friend Eva had her faith tested when, five months after her wedding, she realized her husband had been cheating on her. This betrayal was an excruciatingly painful time for her and her family as they watched her suffer and cry out to God, *Why?* His infidelity was so unexpected. She had known him for five years before marrying him. Both of them had grown up in the church and knew the ways of the Lord. She believed that, since God was in the mix, surely His blessings would follow.

This time was a difficult test of her faith, and it began the very moment she questioned her trust in God. She spiraled into a depression that lasted for years, a seemingly endless season where any hope for future happiness seemed non-existent. She had been robbed of her security, her dreams, and her joy. It seemed impossible for her to ever regain her faith.

God always makes a way for each and every one of us, like He did for Eva. The Book of James also says in verses 5 and 6; *"If any of you lacks wisdom, you should ask God, who gives generously to all without finding fault, and it will be given to you. But when you ask, you must believe and not doubt.."* Sometimes these tests of faith can leave us frozen in our tracks. Wisdom gives us the ability to think and act upon the insights

God gives us. Wisdom may not reveal all the answers we seek but it enables us to actively participate in God's plan for us. Eva went from asking, '*Why?*' and began asking, '*What do you have for me? How do I overcome this?*'

Our Redemption

The good thing about having our faith tested is that God customizes the tests for our own unique story and the lessons He wants us to learn. We each work at a different pace and respond differently to our personalized trials. It took Eva years for her to trust again, to trust herself, to trust God, and to trust love. However, she endured; and because she did, God redeemed her. Little by little, He began to give her back everything she had lost, including a faithful and wonderful new husband who lives out his relationship with Christ. Her endurance also brought forth an adorable baby girl who serves as a constant reminder of God's promises to His faithful ones. Yes, it was a hard test, but with God's extended grace, she passed it. The end of one difficult chapter in her life resulted in an even better new beginning. Looking back now, she can count it all joy.

The trials we go through are anything but joyous in and of themselves, but they can produce a fruit of righteousness in each of us when we change our perspective regarding the situation. As difficult as it may seem, going through a trial often works in our favor when we ask God to make use of it for us. And when our faith has been strengthened and our endurance has grown, there is an even greater assurance of what we will receive in eternity with Him. *"I consider that our present sufferings are not worth comparing with the glory that will be revealed in us."* (Romans 8:18) In heaven, God will give us our full rights as His daughters and sons, with freedom from death, agony, and best of all, freedom from any more tests.

Questions for Reflection

1. What is challenging your faith right now?

2. How have your past difficulties in life provided opportunities for your faith to grow?

3. According to Ephesians 2:8, where does Faith come from?

4. Hebrews 11 is known as the Faith chapter. It records the names and stories of Old Testament heroes. How were these biblical heroes able to accomplish great and powerful things for God?

5. Read Hebrews 11:1: "Now faith is confidence in what we hope for and assurance about what we do not see." What are some things right now that you are hoping for but remain unseen? How is this exercising your faith?

Change

Forget the former things; do not dwell on the past. See, I am doing a new thing! Now it springs up; do you not perceive it? I am making a way in the wilderness and streams in the wasteland.

Isaiah 43:18-19

—*Pastor Lena*

The woman sitting across from me was fidgeting with a lightly chewed pencil. Ruby was nervous about how her kids would take her decision to go back to college and had come to me for advice. She was months away from her 40th birthday; her son and daughter were in 10th and 6th grade, respectively. She had been a dental hygienist for eighteen years and, with her children moving into middle and high school, she had begun to wonder: *What's next? When the kids leave home, what will be left of me?* She decided it was time to end her career in dentistry and embark on nursing school.

Making the decision was one thing, telling her family another. Ruby wanted advice and encouragement on how to share her news with her family. I told her simply, "This is a good thing, your family will understand." She smiled shyly and took a deep breath. Her family would be supportive, but she knew they wouldn't understand the changes ahead for all of them. The kids would need to do more chores to help around the house. Mom would be busy doing homework instead of shuttling them to another sport or activity. There would be more quiet time at the house for everyone to study. It meant a big change, and change is almost always hard.

Ruby's story reminded me of a kid I met when I started my youth ministry internship. Dave was the valedictorian of his high school class—a proud accomplishment for him and his family. They were not a well-to-do family; both parents worked hard to provide. For them, a top school would be out of reach without a scholarship. Dave's accomplishment meant he had full scholarships available for engineering programs at two Florida universities. Dave came to me because he didn't know how to break the news to his parents that he wanted to skip the scholarships and attend a discipleship academy that offered no college credits. Instead, this highly focused academic student wanted a break from his demanding education and wished to dedicate the year to learning more about Jesus. I encouraged Dave to talk with his family and really pray about the options presented to him. He ultimately decided to forfeit the scholarships and devoted the next few years to attending the discipleship academy and traveling to Africa. He was happy pursuing something that spoke to his passion and never regretted following the prescribed path even though it meant a big change for him and his family.

About two years after this conversation with Dave, my roommate, Lauren, told me she was moving out. I enjoyed living with her for the past six months, so this news was disappointing. "I'm pregnant," she said under her breath. "Jason and I decided to get married."

She and her boyfriend met at church while she was still a senior in high school. They had been together for five years and both agreed marriage was in the future, but Jason had wanted to wait a while longer.

Her eyes filled with tears. "It's just . . . It's just not supposed to be in this order. What will my parents think when they find out? They will be so disappointed!" Her new reality was very different from all the dreams she'd had—her scrapbook filled with wedding ideas she'd kept since she was a little girl and the traditional path of marriage first, children second, had both flown right out the window.

All I could do for Lauren was pray. We asked God to give her peace, clarity, and direction in her life. Lauren's sudden change in circumstances wasn't planned but it also wasn't something she could avoid. I encouraged her to tell her family the next day so that they could help her through the transitions. They received the news with a reserved disappointment and excitement about their first grandchild. The couple had a small, simple wedding before starting their new life as a family.

Ruby, Dave, and Lauren were experiencing the same thing: change. Things for all three of them would change drastically in their life and in the lives of their families. Each person's change moved them from one season in their lives to the next. Whatever change that they were about to experience, whether the change was planned like it was for Ruby and Dave or came to them suddenly like Lauren's, this change was all at God's hands. And the only way to get through it was by trusting in Him.

Change is Expected

God set "change" in place in Genesis 8:22, *"As long as the earth endures, seedtime and harvest, cold and heat, summer and winter, day and night will never cease."* Change of seasons, change of time, and change in us is spoken about throughout the Bible. Ecclesiastes 3:1-22 gives a thorough explanation of change. King Solomon, who wrote Ecclesiastes, was the wealthiest person of all time, even compared to today's standards of wealth. He was also known as the wisest king in the Bible. He paints a very good picture of change by comparing the seasons to the swings of emotions and changes in actions in our lives. King Solomon wanted us, the readers, to know change is not always something geographic or time-based, but rather about changes of action. Ecclesiastes 3:3 says, *"A time to kill and a time to heal, a time to tear down and a time to build,"* while verse 6 adds, *"A time to search and a time to give up, a time to keep and a time to throw away."*

There are two things seen throughout scripture about change. We first see that it will happen, no matter what. We will always experience change in our lives. We are not born with the intention we remain a baby; we are destined to grow. (Luke 2:40) **God also confirms in scripture that every season of change is in His control and that no change in our lives is outside the bounds of His power. (Daniel 2:21 & Ecclesiastes 3:1)** Change is inevitable, and God is in charge, so the scripture is there to prepare us for that and to give us an image of what change can look like, as well as what can happen when it does. Change will come—but the way we respond to that change is up to us.

Change is an Opportunity

God also means for us to prepare for those changes, giving us an opportunity to prove our faithfulness to Him. Just as fall means farmers start to gather the last of the crops in the field and then clean and lock away their equipment, or cities prepare for the winter ahead by cleaning out storm drains, performing maintenance on snow removal equipment, and stockpiling extra fuel for extended blackouts, we are meant to prepare for the trials ahead. The comparisons made in Ecclesiastes are there for us to understand we need to be ready when things happen in our lives.

By recognizing what season we are in, we can prepare for the next. Ruby and Dave knew change was happening. They recognized the change of season in their life and planned for the possibilities to come and the new directions they would take. The change was scary for Ruby because she knew the challenges her family might experience with her return to school. Dave knew the disappointment his family would feel for choosing not to go to college. Neither one of them just "let life happen". Both took time to prepare and made plans that helped to slowly remove any anxiety and uncertainty while giving them confidence to venture into that next season.

Lauren's sudden change in season caught her off guard that meant a shift in her lifestyle, finances, personal time, and her romantic relationship. When change comes suddenly, like it did for Lauren, we must turn to the Bible to help us prepare. Romans 8:28 says, "*And we know that in all things God works for the good of those who love him, who have been called according to his purpose.*" God will always work it out for our good as long as we pray in the spirit. (Romans 8:26-27)

One of the most heartening scriptures regarding change is Proverbs 3:5-6: "*Trust in the Lord with all your heart; do not depend on your own understanding.*

Seek his will in all you do, and he will show you which path to take." We need to trust that God is in control of the unknown season ahead of us.

You may have experienced a sudden change in your own life such as the death of a loved one, loss of a job, a divorce, or an unexpected diagnosis. We may walk into these moments feeling unprepared. However, we must trust that the season God has placed us in, whether it is sudden or planned, is all in God's control. Even if the change in your season brings heartache and sadness, trust God as your comforter in those times. **Trust that God can turn a season that seems messy and destructive into something incredible.**

That new, incredible season can be a testimony to those around you, just as it says in Ecclesiastes 3:11, *"He has made everything beautiful in its time."* Every season has a purpose in your life, so prepare for the changes you see coming and lean on and trust in God when unexpected moments happen in your life. He is there to hold your hand—all you have to do is reach for Him.

Questions for Reflection

1. What is the season you are in now? Would you describe it as planned, unexpected, destructive, sudden, or wilderness?

2. Think back on a season that came on you suddenly. What were the lessons or stories you took away from that season?

3. When preparing for a new season in your life, have you looked ahead to it with joy and expectation or hesitation and anxiety? Why?

4. Read Ecclesiastes 3:1-22. What are your favorite three comparisons?

5. Read Galatians 6:9. Think of a time when you felt like a hamster on a wheel—working hard and getting nowhere. Maybe you worked at a job for a miserable boss, or went through a messy divorce, or attended a college class that you did not understand. What does this verse say about that season in your life?

6. Read Isaiah 43:18-19. What new thing has God yet to do in your life?

Compassion

Therefore, as God's chosen people, holy and dearly loved, clothe yourselves with compassion, kindness, humility, gentleness and patience.

Colossians 3:12

—Pastor Lucy

Compassion. We all know it when we see it, but we don't all always have it in our hearts or offer it to others. My good friend Sharon, however, fits the image of compassion. She's that person you can call anytime you have a problem and she will figure out a way to help you. If it's beyond her, she'll volunteer her husband or find someone else. She has generously given away material things like cars and money. However, the best part is that she is constantly giving of herself through her gifts and talents. She's quiet and meek, but lively spirited when it comes to helping others in need. At the same time, she knows the difference between someone who is genuinely in need and one merely trying to take advantage. She is always there to help someone who wants a hand-up, not just a hand-out.

Sharon's church is located in Tampa's inner city, where vagabonds and drifters often stand on street corners asking for money or food, and she goes out of her way to help these people. However, the ones who capture her heart are the people and families who come to her church seeking help: Single moms struggling to pay their bills and living without electricity. Families who have been forced to ration the little food they have left in their cupboards until their food stamps are replenished. Children wearing tattered clothes, who just want something nice to wear to school.

Sharon understands these people because she was once in the same position. She was that family. She was that child. Sharon went from having limited resources to having nothing at all. On the flip side of the coin, she has also been in the position of abundance and having deep gratitude. Because she understands need, she offers help, hope for a better future, and an overflowing well of compassion.

The Example of Jesus

In the Gospel of Matthew, chapter 9 tells us Jesus felt compassion towards the crowds around Him because He saw and understood that they were confused and helpless, much like sheep without a shepherd. He had compassion for the hungry, who had sat for three days and were unable to eat after eagerly listening to Him teach. (See Mark 8:2)

Like all of us, Jesus felt grief and pain. Following the news of the beheading of His cousin, John the Baptist, Jesus went away to be alone. However, the people found Him and when He saw that they needed him, He set His grief aside and healed the sick (see Matthew 14:13-14). **There are multiple examples in the Bible of Jesus caring for others before Himself.** Jesus was not only attentive to people in need but He always responded with unconditional love. At the end of His life, Jesus showed His love and the ultimate compassion toward all humanity when He hung on the cross and died for our sins. (Luke 23:33) Even then, He asked for mercy for the people He loved. "*Father, forgive them, for they know not what they do.*" (Luke 23:34) Jesus was and is compassion.

Choose Your Spiritual Outfit

Every morning, when we get out of bed and start our day, most of us begin by choosing what outfit we're going to wear. We base it on the weather, our mood, and what we have planned for that day. But what if, instead of worrying whether those pants went with that sweater, we worried about whether our outfit was the best for our spiritual selves.

Jesus taught us to wear a spiritual outfit of compassion and kindness to those around us, at all times and in as many ways as possible. In Colossians 3:12, Paul presents the five basic wardrobe essentials for all people: compassion, kindness, humility, gentleness, and patience. However, it's up to us to decide whether or not we are going to clothe ourselves with such qualities. We are instructed to be compassionate, but in the end the choice is ours. Much like the commandment to love our neighbor as ourselves (Mark 12:31), the decision to live with compassion in our hearts is ours.

What would living with compassion look like? It would mean being intentional about the people with whom we surround ourselves, as well as those who walk alongside us in this wonderful journey called life. It means being aware of the need that surrounds us every day and pausing in our busy days to offer a hand, a word of solace, or to simply offer some support. It would mean extending grace to others, just as our Heavenly Father does every day.

Look for someone who needs your help today. Don't worry about whether they can pay you back or whether they will appreciate your help. **Compassion is about doing for others without expecting anything in return—not even a thank you.** It is doing for others because Christ did for us. It is caring for other people and striving to make a difference, even in a world that is corrupt, greedy, and selfish.

Show Compassion Where You Are

Sharon is someone who makes a difference right where she stands. She started a simple ministry at her church, designed to inspire volunteers and help empower those who are helpless, hopeless, broken, or hurt. She knew she couldn't fill all those needs on her own, so she created an army of sorts to help her, just as Jesus did with His disciples. These people are the hands and feet of Jesus.

Her ministry, known as Thrive, helps people from the community with all kinds of physical, emotional, and spiritual needs. She offers resources for jobs, including workshops, trainings, assistance, grants, counseling, and more. In addition, Thrive offers one-on-one meetings, prayers, and guidance. They also offer the simpler things like groceries, childcare, and clothing. By partnering with several non-profit services within the community, Thrive can expand its reach and also offer specialized services. The main goal is to help people become self-sufficient, instead of settling for taking handouts for the rest of their lives. Sharon's mission to extend compassion has opened the door for dozens of other families to go from crisis to stability, to break away from helplessness and embrace hopefulness.

When we are selfless in our actions, we give an incredible gift to others. Compassion is more than just a feeling—it's a feeling that produces action. When we respond with compassion, no matter how small, Jesus will bless it and multiply it. Too often in the rush of life, we picture others as being in the way of our progress. We get frustrated with the woman taking her time at the grocery store, the person who is driving under the speed limit in the left lane, or the harried mother with noisy kids. Instead of allowing the irritation to take over, why not extend compassion instead? Show patience. **Look for the why behind the what**. Maybe the woman in the grocery store is having trouble seeing. Maybe that driver is distracted by some bad news she just received. Maybe the mom is at the end of her rope and needs a short break. How can we help these people instead of ignoring them or worrying only about ourselves?

We have become so self-absorbed with our personal agendas and our own needs that we miss out on hundreds of opportunities every day to show compassion and help someone else thrive. So choose your spiritual outfit wisely and make sure you are displaying outwardly what you, as a Christian, already believe inwardly. Our world needs more compassion and our world needs us to deliver that gift, just as Jesus did for all of us.

Questions for Reflection

1. Who are some of the most compassionate people you know and why do you see them as compassionate?

2. Do you think that one's motivation for showing compassion matters? Why or why not?

3. What are some ways that you can be more compassionate?

4. Romans 13:14 says: *"Rather, clothe yourselves with the Lord Jesus Christ, and do not think about how to gratify the desires of the flesh."* How will you clothe yourself with the Lord today?

Relationships

My command is this: Love each other as I have loved you. Greater love has no one than this: to lay down one's life for one's friends.

John 15:12-13

—Pastor Lena

I learned a hard lesson about relationships and trust when my best friend stole a hundred dollars from me. I was in middle school and Katie had been my best friend for a couple of years. We'd met in church and became instant friends. My mother warned me that something seemed different about Katie and she worried Katie might hurt me. All I saw was Katie, a girl who seemed to badly need a friend.

Katie came from a very different home than my own. I was too young to realize all the differences, but her family was troubled, which had a huge impact on Katie. People made fun of Katie because she didn't dress the same or act the same as everyone else. Maybe to fit in, or maybe because she had some emotional issues, Katie told tall tales. One time, she said she thought she was pregnant even though she'd never had sex. I knew enough to know that was impossible unless you were the Virgin Mary. She talked about seeing Tupac Shakur, the famous murdered rapper. She believed he was alive and that she'd seen him waiting at a red light in her small Florida town. I excused her behavior as somebody who was crying out for a friend and I wanted to be that friend for Katie, the one person she could count on.

On my birthday, she spent the night at my house. I showed her my favorite gift from my parents: a "Dear Diary" personal organizer. Pink with sparkles around the edge, the portable diary needed a password to open. I shared all this with Katie—she was my best friend after all—but after Katie left the next day, I couldn't find the diary anywhere.

Katie stole it. When I confronted her, she lied and said she didn't have it but I knew better. Still, I didn't let it ruin my friendship with her and I kept inviting her over. The next time Katie spent the night at my house, she stole $100 from me. I was hurt and shocked that my best friend would steal from me, and then deny it and lie to my face. After that, I finally started to distance myself from her.

Choose Relationships Wisely

I am a 'people person' and tend to be warm and open. I make friends easily and have a wide network I can call on when I need them. Yet as much as I love meeting new people, the hard truth is that not everyone deserves the emotional investment necessary to form a relationship.

Relationships can enhance your life or hurt it. It's up to you to choose the people in your life using wisdom and foresight. Katie was my first betrayal by a friend, but as I entered my teen years I experienced one betrayal after another, as many teen girls do once boys enter the picture. In an effort to be accepted and to have as many friends as possible, I lowered my personal standards and accepted things that I shouldn't have. I repeated the mistakes I made with Katie, allowing people to lie to me and excusing bad behavior in an effort to keep the peace. It wasn't just girl friends who betrayed me; it was boyfriends, too. Over and over, I was hurt because I accepted unhealthy relationships and maintained them regardless of what it cost me personally.

It wasn't until I realized those relationships were more draining than fulfilling that I began making better choices. My attitude started to change and I began to question all my relationships, even good friendships. I became more mistrusting and sarcastic, like I was putting a wall up against being hurt. When I entered college, I finally put a lot of distance between the toxic relationships of my past and myself. That's when things truly began to change.

God's Opinion on Relationships

God has made it abundantly clear how our connections with other people should work. In His eyes, relationships should always be encouraging, uplifting, strengthening, and mutually beneficial. Friendship is best defined in John 15:12-13: *"My command is this: Love each other as I have loved you. Greater love has no one than this: to lay down one's life for one's friends."* Relationships need to be based on love—a love without judgment or preconceived ideas. For example, when I first befriended Katie, I did so regardless of what others said. However, when it became clear that being friends with her was not uplifting me, but rather hurting me, I had to let her go. Proverbs 17:17 states *"A friend loves at all times, and a brother is born for a time of adversity."* A relationship that meets God's standards will always uplift and encourage you to be a better person, as Proverbs 27:17 says, *"As iron sharpens iron, so one person sharpens another."*

In the Bible, the best example of friendship is seen between Jonathan, the son of King Saul, and David. King Saul was an evil, ruthless, and diabolical man who killed his own people. However, his son Jonathan was kindhearted and was best friends with David. David was one of King Saul's soldiers and servants, and the future King of Israel. We see just how close their friendship becomes in 1 Samuel 18:6-9 when King Saul grows jealous of David and plots to kill him. However, it is Saul's son, Jonathan, who helps save David's life. (1 Samuel 19, 20, 21)

The book of Proverbs has several scriptures regarding relationships we can use as a guideline to choose the right people for our life. "*Walk with the wise and become wise, for a companion of fools suffers harm.*" (Proverbs 13:20)

The Bible warns against friendships with fools—Katie and my high school boyfriends were those fools and I should have steered clear. We see another warning on the types of relationships to avoid in 2 Corinthians 6:14, "*Do not be yoked together with unbelievers. For what do righteousness and wickedness have in common? Or what fellowship can light have with darkness?*" A yoke is a heavy, metal necklace-like piece of equipment used to bind two oxen together. It forced the team to move in the same direction at the same time, preventing them from moving in whichever direction they wanted. In this verse, the yoke is a close relationship between two people, where they become so intermingled they are essentially bound together. The scripture warns to avoid close relationships with unbelievers because your life's direction won't match that of a person living in wickedness.

In my friendship with Katie, I walked in righteousness—I believed in truth, honesty, fairness, and forgiveness—and I was willing to lay down my life for my friend. I wasn't perfect, but I tried to love her and support her at all times. However, Katie was living with wickedness and sin in her heart, which came out by her constant lying, stealing, and other things the Bible warns against. The "yoke" attaching me to Katie disintegrated because my life was on a path seeking truth and honoring God, while Katie wanted to live a life that did *not* honor God. My dating relationships were the same; I was not in an equal relationship with any of those guys. Our futures, moral standards, and relationships with God were not moving in the same direction. It wasn't until I looked to the Bible and God as an example and guidance with respect to my relationships that I found people who truly made me a better person and a better Christian.

Some of us avoid relationships altogether because we don't want to be hurt. That choice is also against the plan God has for your life, as we are built to be in relationships. He desires for us to succeed in relationships, and in order to succeed we must follow the guidelines put in place throughout the Bible. Learn to love and not judge, recognize when you are in the company of fools, and un-yoke yourself from people who are not moving you forward in life. Most of all, maintain a strong relationship with God and Christ. In Their loving spirit you will find the best relationship of all, one you can depend upon in the darkest and brightest of days.

Questions for Reflection

1. Can you think of the first friendship betrayal that happened in your life? How did you forgive and move on from that hurt?

2. How do you choose your friends? Have you set up boundaries or non-negotiable terms in your friendships?

3. Who are the five people you surround yourself with? Do you believe these five people are helping you move your life forward to fulfill your goals?

4. Read Proverbs 13:20. Would you consider the people in your current relationships (friendships, romantic, or business) wise or foolish?

5. Read 2 Corinthians 6:14. Can you identify a relationship when you were yoked to someone else? Did you both move in the same direction in life?

6. Read 1 Samuel 18:1-5 and Chapters 19 & 20. Can you identify the Jonathan in your life?

Insecurity

*There is no fear in love,
but perfect love casts out fear.*

I John 4:18

—Pastor Lucy

Insecurity is like a prison, one that so many of us get caught in and struggle to escape. There was a time in my life when I felt like I was trapped in my own body and mind. I was too scared to step out and be myself because I was worried people would reject me. For the most part, I kept my thoughts and feelings to myself. I decided my ideas and dreams were foolish before I even attempted to voice them. Ultimately, I defined myself as insignificant in this massive and magnificent world.

I did everything I could to go unnoticed and not draw any attention to myself because I worried I wouldn't meet the expectations of others and thus be subjected to the sting of criticism, rejection, or feelings of worthlessness. So, I dressed to go unnoticed. I didn't wear anything too colorful or fashionable for fear of drawing attention. I spoke very little to avoid any type of conflict or tension. In short, I wasn't myself once I walked out the doors of my house.

Home was the only place where I felt safe enough to "test the waters" with my voice, but even then there were times when I felt like I was met with disappointment. Literally and figuratively, I sat in the back of the room, choosing to play it safe by keeping my distance from anyone who could potentially hurt me.

I married my college sweetheart, Tommy Kyllonen, and together we entered ministry life. He began as a youth pastor at Crossover Church and I began working as a teen counselor and juvenile probation officer. At the same time, we started a new youth ministry from scratch, a group that grew to hundreds of teens. It seemed like a perfect fit because Tommy and I both had a heart for the youth ministry, specifically inner-city youth. Many of these teens came from the housing projects in our community and knew nothing but dysfunction and brokenness. God used both of us to show them what normal could look like.

On the surface, everything seemed great, but secretly I was having a hard time managing all of the attention and my new title of "Youth Pastor's Wife". As much as I tried, I couldn't go totally unnoticed; people within the ministry constantly sought me out for advice, for friendship, or for my connections. All the attention I had always avoided was suddenly right there in front of me. I didn't know what to do other than flounder along to keep from drowning in my own insecurities.

Six years later, Tommy became the Lead Pastor of our church, and "Pastor's Wife" became my new title, which meant leadership in front of the entire church. Surely, I thought, God had made a mistake. As much as I supported my husband, deep down I believed I wouldn't be able to live up to everyone else's expectations. Until then, I had managed to stay under the radar and mostly in the shadows, but I knew I could no longer get away with that. **I watched as God began to bring light into the inner darkness I had created.**

Around this same time, my husband convinced me to join a women's small group for the first time. This was a turning point in my life. It allowed me to learn who I was, and who God is. Merriam-Webster defines *insecurity* as: *deficient in assurance: beset by fear and anxiety*. For me, that summed up my life. Even though I was in college to get my master's degree in mental health counseling, I was deficient in assurance of my purpose and myself. I was deficient in assurance of the totality of God's Word. I lived in fear of the unknown and of what other people said or thought of me. Insecurity had become one of my personality traits—and it was affecting every area of my life. I finally grew tired of feeling inadequate and of trying to mask those feelings.

Believe You are a Princess of God's Kingdom

I longed for the same confidence I saw in other brave and fearless women. Subsequently, this longing took me on a search of the Bible and of myself. I learned that our actions are a result of our sense of identity, not the other way around. **Meaning, the way we perceive ourselves, and those around us, determines the decisions we make and how we act.**

Imagine, for instance, a young girl who believes she is a princess. She puts on her favorite dress, dons a tiara, and slips into her mom's high heels. She starts to dance in front of a mirror without reservation because she believes she is a beautiful princess. That belief is directing her behavior, her heartfelt song, and her dance. She isn't shy or holding back—she is a princess in that moment. God loves us all as we are, and sees us as magnificently and wonderfully made. In His eyes, we are all princesses (or princes). We need to believe that and live as if we believe Him.

When I truly made this realization, I began the journey of correcting the false self-perception that had led to my insecurities. I based my new confidence on the knowledge that God is who He says He is and I am who He says I am.

God tells me in His Word that I am a masterpiece and that I was created with a purpose. *"For we are God's masterpiece. He has created us anew in Christ Jesus, so we can do the good things He planned for us long ago."*

(Ephesians 2:10) Most women tend to think that there is nothing extraordinary about us, but that is contrary to the way God thinks. As a matter of fact, no one has my same exact fingerprint, no one has the same exact DNA as me, and at the end of the day, there is only one me!

I hid inside myself for too many years instead of celebrating who I was and how God saw me. When I did that, I grew closer to Him and felt even more of His love. Read with me as David, the Psalmist, opens himself up to the Lord as he realizes he cannot escape from His love:

> 1 *You have searched me, Lord,*
>   and you know me.
>
> *2 You know when I sit and when I rise;*
>   you perceive my thoughts from afar.
>
> *7 Where can I go from your Spirit?*
>   Where can I flee from your presence?
>
> *11 If I say, "Surely the darkness will hide me*
>   *and the light become night around me,"*
>
> *12 Even the darkness will not be dark to you;*
>   *the night will shine like the day,*
>   *for darkness is as light to you.*
>
> *13 For you created my inmost being;*
>   you knit me together in my mother's womb.

> *14 I praise you because I am fearfully and wonderfully made;*
>   your works are wonderful,
>   I know that full well.
>
> *23 Search me, God, and know my heart;*
>   test me and know my anxious thoughts.
>
> *24 See if there is any offensive way in me,*
>   and lead me in the way everlasting.
>
> (Psalm 139)

David can't escape from the God who created him, so he invites God into his heart and into his thoughts. He knows that God was the author of his life and that God designed him, and the plan for David's life, fearfully and wonderfully! As I read these words, I experienced a mental shift and invited God to invade my personal space. **When I did, He began to whisper that I had been carefully crafted with purpose, intent, and worth.**

Instead of trying to figure everything out on my own, I can seek Him and discover more of who I am. Before I came into existence, God created me with skills, talents, ideas, and gifts to use for His purpose. The problem? Like many women, I focused on what I couldn't do, instead of what I could. I focused on what I was not, instead of who I am. This contrast reminds me of a quote by Nicole Unice, author of the book, *She's Got Issues*: "Comparison is healthy when it challenges me to be a better person; it's toxic when it tells me who I am as a person."

From Insecurity to Security

Having an intimate relationship with God was my bridge as I crossed over from scattered insecurities to Godly security! There is freedom in knowing that the one who matters most, and the one who loves me as I am, is my Creator. My security comes in knowing that He is secure. He is just. He is Faithful. He is constant—and that's a relief! My friends, circumstances, and thoughts can take all kinds of twists, turns, and dead ends, but I take comfort in knowing I can anchor the insecurities of this life to God's Word and His promises to me.

Security has become my new way of life. I now feel safe, stable, and free from my self-perceived fears and anxieties. Because of this newfound security, I found my inner voice. I have been blessed to share a platform with my pastor husband through our church, and now I can actively live out my mission in life: to create empowering opportunities for women to intimately know who God is and who He says they are—secure. **When we fix our minds on God's Word as our one and only true source of our identity, our feelings will follow.** This, in turn, will lead to healthier, purpose-driven decisions in our lives. We become confident of better and greater things and we invite others to experience this assurance for themselves.

Questions for Reflection

1. How has confidence or doubt in your life affected your decision-making?

2. Have you invested time and energy in things (people, places or things) other than God in pursuit of security? Explain.

3. What are some truths from God's Word that you need to remind yourself of?

4. Focus on the positive qualities in your life. Take a blank sheet of paper and ask the Lord to guide you in an honest assessment of your traits. You might be surprised at what God shows you about yourself.

Failure

Trust in the Lord with all your heart, and lean not on your own understanding; in all your ways submit to Him, and He will make your paths straight.

Proverbs 3:5-6

—*Pastor Lena*

"I can't believe this is happening again," said my friend Kathy. Tears were in her eyes and I could see her hesitation to share the truth. I waited, sitting across from her at the dining room table. Dinner was growing cold, but this was far more important. The whole thing had started with a simple question—where's your husband?

Kathy took a deep breath. "I haven't seen him in five days. He's been clean for three years. He was working again. We were starting to save money to get a new car. I had started to pay off the credit card debt. He even talked about going back to school." She choked back a sob and shook her head. "I can't believe he's on this path again."

From the start, Kathy and her husband had a rocky marriage, due in part to his addictions to cocaine and marijuana. They had been married for five years, and when she'd said her vows she knew he had a drug problem, but trusted he had it under control. He didn't. Soon after they got married, money from their bank account started disappearing—money he was using to pay for prostitutes and drugs. When Kathy found out, she debated leaving but she loved her husband and hoped he would change. They went to counseling, and he went to rehab. But like many addicts, recovery was a stop-and-start process, and her husband relapsed as soon as he was out of rehab.

For the first two years of their marriage, Kathy rode the rollercoaster of living with an addict. Her husband couldn't keep a job and they struggled to pay their bills because she was the only one working. Every time she got paid, he would siphon off whatever he could to pay for drugs.

Like many addicts, he didn't just abuse drugs—he drove intoxicated, he stole and pawned things taken from his home and from family members, and he made hundreds of bad decisions. When he hit his true rock bottom, her husband went to their pastor who helped him find a rehab clinic. Her husband was committed this time and determined to make it work. He stayed sober for three years.

Then, in spectacular fashion, he fell off the wagon. Kathy wasn't sure what the trigger was, but something happened the night they'd gone out with a few people from work. She'd gone to bed early and woke up in the middle of the night. Hearing sounds in the living room, she caught her husband having sex with a coworker on the couch. Drug paraphernalia was spread all over the floor. "He was so high he didn't even see me standing there," she said.

My heart broke. I was so sure that they had been on the right track, that God was turning things around in their life.

Kathy was at a loss. She didn't know which way to turn or what decision to make next. "I know **God hates divorce but my husband hates commitment,**" **she said.** "I feel like God has failed me."

She thought God should have warned her or sent her husband a message. Kathy was adrift and feeling abandoned by God. We prayed together, but after we finished I knew I had to tell her the truth, which most people don't want to hear. "Life is choice driven," I shook my head. "God did not fail you. You failed God when you neglected His word before you guys got married. You didn't heed the warning from your family when they told you not to marry him because he was still doing drugs." I quoted 2 Corinthians 6:14 to her, and reminded my friend that she and her husband were unequally yoked and that they were going in two different directions.

The words were hard for me to say and even harder for her to hear, but I knew this wasn't the time to coddle her or go along with her pity party. Both of them had made mistakes and she needed to see that. **Too often, we blame God when we fail at something in life, when in reality we are just seeing the results of our choices.**

Kathy confronted her husband and gave him an ultimatum—go to rehab or leave the house. In the end, he chose to leave and filed for divorce. Even though she was devastated, she accepted his choice and moved on. Kathy is now married to another man and they have three beautiful boys together. Her ex-husband is still struggling to get his life together.

When I Fail in Life

Everything that happens in life is a result of the choices we make. The Bible talks about seedtime and harvest time. We plant the seeds with our decisions and reap the results, both good and bad. *"Do not be deceived: God cannot be mocked. A man reaps what he sows. Whoever sows to please their flesh, from the flesh will reap destruction; whoever sows to please the Spirit, from the Spirit will reap eternal life. Let us not become weary in doing good, for at the proper time we will reap a harvest if we do not give up."* (Galatians 6:7-9)

We need to learn to not sow seeds of failure in our lives so we don't see a harvest of failure later. How do we do that? **By making sure our lives align with the Word.** The Bible is there to provide basic instructions for us to follow before leaving this Earth. It's a handbook on how to live a life submitting to God's perfect will. Too many people don't want to live according to the Bible or God's instructions, so when things go wrong they blame God.

Maybe you feel like a failure because of a failed marriage or a financial crisis. Look back at your choices and see how they led to this situation. Did you take on too much credit card debt? Buy more house than you could afford? Spend more than you made? **The failure isn't that God didn't provide—it's that you weren't judicious with the resources God did give you.**

Some parents feel like they have failed if their kids aren't star students, or amazing athletes, or if they have behavioral problems. I see parents come to resent God for "not answering their prayers" to fix their kids. As a pastor, I help parents discover the seeds they may have unwittingly planted along the way. Maybe parents withheld discipline in order to be the child's best friend. Maybe the parents were divorced and dragged their drama in front of the children causing psychological triggers. Parents allow their personal success and busy-ness to keep them from staying up-to-date with their child's circle of friends, grades, or interests, and then the parents are shocked to learn their child joined a gang. All of the seeds harvested in our life are rooted in the choices we have made or the choices others have made that impacted our lives.

What Can God Do with My Failures?

Everything.

Proverbs 3:5-6 says, *"Trust in the Lord with all your heart, and lean not on your own understanding; in all your ways submit to Him, and He will make your paths straight."* A lot of folks miss the *"in all your ways submit to Him"* part in that verse. Human nature makes us want to live life without acknowledging that God is in control, but you need to be firm with yourself and resist the urge to forget who is in the driver's seat.

Trusting that God is in control means leaning on Him in everything. Jesus says, *"I am the vine; you are the branches. If you remain in Me and I in you, you will bear much fruit; apart from Me you can do nothing."* (John 15:5) Much of what we endure can be avoided if we follow the words of Jesus, and we can only follow Him by abiding in Him. We must trust His words, *"So is My word that goes out from My mouth: It will not return to Me empty, but will accomplish what I desire and achieve the purpose for which I sent it."* (Isaiah 55:11) God's Word is already established. Trust it. *"Heaven and earth shall pass away, but My words will never pass away."* (Matthew 24:35)

Look at the Word of God as a plumb line. It keeps you on the straight path and helps you avoid failure. Spend time with the Bible daily to build trust in the words God has given to us. **He has planted the seeds we need, so if we allow them to take root in our hearts and tend to them as they bloom, our harvest will be much richer and more bountiful.**

Questions for Reflection

1. What would you say was the biggest failure in your life?

2. Think of a time when you failed at something. What choices did you make that took you down that path that resulted in failure?

3. What good seeds could you start to sow now in your life?

4. Read Galatians 6:7-9. What are some ways you sow to the flesh? What are some ways we sow to the spirit?

5. What current failure are you trying to overcome? Find three scriptures you can pray over and believe in to help you counteract that failure.

6. Read John 15:1-17. Jesus talks about "abiding in the vine". How does He say we need to abide in the vine? Would you say you are abiding in the vine, or are you acting like a branch about to be cut off?

Guilt & Shame

Those who look to Him are radiant;
their faces are never covered with shame.

Psalm 34:5

—Pastor Lucy

Oscar Wilde once wrote, "The only difference between the saint and the sinner is that every saint has a past, and every sinner has a future."

Each of us has a story. Our stories are flavored with our unique experiences and our various backgrounds, cultures, and traditions. Much of our past and upbringing contributes to who we are today and whom we choose to become. This means that our past, with all of its experiences, challenges, journeys, memories, etc., will continue to influence us in different ways through our lifetime. The danger is found when we get stuck in our past and become mired in a traumatic event, experience, or memory.

Difficulty letting go makes it impossible to move on and experience all the blessings that God has for us.

Some of us choose to remain stuck and ruminate unceasingly about the past over something or someone that cannot be changed. Whether someone wronged us or we did something wrong, we can choose to let it haunt us or we can choose to let it go. As crazy as it may sound, it's often easier to let it haunt us and keep it alive in our thoughts than to let the issue go and surrender it to God. The latter would require us to relinquish control of it and too many of us would rather enjoy the feeling of control and having actual control (refer back to the Control chapter).

The Truth About Guilt and Shame

As a result of some of our decisions, too many people are living with feelings of worthlessness, shame, guilt, holding grudges, etc., over things that happened in their unresolved pasts. This creates a barrier—a disconnect from our loving, forgiving Heavenly Father. We have all carelessly said something hurtful or done something terrible, maybe even unspeakable, that we later sincerely regretted. Yet, what we do with that regret is sometimes more important than the incident itself.

God wants and is able to redeem us, but His adversary the enemy prefers to keep us stuck in our past. One of his favorite methods is using guilt and shame to keep us down and hold us back from

God's loving arms. Nonetheless, there is a difference between these two words. Guilt is when we realize our past mistake or failure. Feelings of guilt can actually be healthy for us because they can reflect our current state of sin and move us towards an attitude of repentance and restoration. However, the enemy will trick us with false guilt to remind us of our transgression and keep us feeling guilty long after we have already been forgiven and the incident forgotten by God. It's actually a promise to us in Isaiah 43:25 "*I—yes, I alone—will blot out your sins for My own sake and will never think of them again.*"

On the other hand, meditating on false guilt will eventually turn into shame. Consider this, "While guilt is rooted in what we have done, shame is the condemnation of *who we are*." (Dr. Juli Slattery and Ginger Taddeo in "Sex and Shame: Your Past Does Not Define You" in *Today's Christian Woman*).

Shame, on the other hand, is the feeling of seeing yourself as a failure because of what you have done. Guilt can prompt you to look at the sin, but shame causes you to look at the sin and the affect it has on your self-identity. Hence, this is a perfect recipe for sabotaging a healthy relationship with God, with yourself, and with others.

First, Forgive Yourself

Katrina is from the Netherlands, a very liberal and tolerant country when it comes to religion, politics, and sex. Dutch women and men live a very free life where they have the freedom to choose to do whatever they want in regards to drugs, relationships, and sex. Prostitution is legal. Katrina spent her whole childhood in Amsterdam where her loving single mother raised her and her younger brother. As a teen, she always knew she wanted to study abroad in the United States upon completing high school. Her dream was to study Psychology while pursuing Dance and end up in a big city like New York or Los Angeles working for a major dance company. But the unexpected happened during her senior year of high school—Katrina got pregnant. In that moment her world came crashing down as a whirlwind of questions and thoughts flooded her mind. Would she have to give up her lifelong dream of becoming a dancer and moving to America?

Katrina refused to panic and decided to remain focused and determined. No one was going to keep her from her dreams—not even a baby. So, she had an abortion with little regard to what her mother or boyfriend thought of her decision. Problem solved. Or so she thought.

Katrina made it to the United States and pursued her degrees in psychology and dance. Her past, however, kept haunting her with guilt, shame, and regret. She tried to escape her memories by staying busy but the feelings persisted. In 2012, while on her first mission trip to Africa, Katrina couldn't hold the truth in any longer. She was talking to a small group and she finally revealed the truth about her abortion. She had been wrestling with her feelings of worthlessness while serving hungry children in a third world country and knew she had to confess to begin to feel whole again.

When she returned home, she began to process and deal with her secret guilt and shame. She received counseling and mentoring that led her to experience true freedom and a new intimacy with God, something she had been lacking. Katrina was able to forgive herself and let it go. In turn, God provided an opportunity for her to help other women who also were in bondage to their guilt and shame.

Katrina facilitated an eight-week Bible study on overcoming the brokenness that abortion leaves behind. God used her discomfort to set her free. He allowed her to go through the mess she created in her life and then use it as a redemptive message to all women who choose to trust in a redeeming God. He made all things work for her good. (Romans 8:28)

Katrina's healing and restoration began when finally admitted the truth about the abortion and spoke about it. She confessed it, acknowledging her brokenness and responsibility in it. She decided to let it go, to forgive herself and believe that God forgave her and was not holding a grudge against her.

While the enemy wants to keep you in bondage to your past, God wants to raise you out of the guilt and shame and clothe you with healing and redemption. **As the enemy plants seeds to make you think that**

God is mad at you, God wants you to know that He takes delight in you and that absolutely nothing can separate you from His love for you. (Romans 8:39)

In addition to this great news, the truth is that your past does not define you! You are not defined by how many men you have slept with or how much you had to drink last night. You are not defined by your addiction, the lies you have told, or the secret sins that you wrestle with. No! It is God who defines you as his precious daughter, His chosen one.

We can't change the past, but God gives us the strength and the power to release it. Katrina, will meet her precious baby in heaven one day. This knowledge keeps her going and motivates her to continue reaching out to women. If you are dealing with guilt and shame, forgive yourself, confess to another, and then allow God's forgiveness to move you towards redemption from your past and hope for your future.

Questions for Reflection

1. What are some lies from the enemy that you have believed and allowed to impact your life?

2. When was the last time you let someone down? How do you feel about it now?

3. Read Romans 8:1-4. How are Christians to deal with this heightened sense of shame and guilt that has resulted from their faith in Jesus and the gospel?

4. Read 2 Corinthians 6:17-18; 1 John 3:1; Romans 8:17. Who does God say you are? How will you live this out?

Fear

For the Spirit God gave us does not make us timid, but gives us power, love, and self-discipline.
                                        2 Timothy 1:7

—Pastor Lena

Fear can take on many forms. It can start with a small seed planted with one event, and grow into something that overtakes your life and robs you of joy and peace. For me, the fear that governed much of my life started in a fast food bathroom when I was seven years old.

"Eww! What's wrong with her!?" A stranger came up to my mother in that bathroom, horrified at the issues I was having, issues that had me constantly running to a restroom. I was in pain almost every single day, and had been since I was four.

What that stranger failed to realize that day in the restroom was that my mother and I had just left the gastrointestinal doctor's office, for yet another visit about the ulcerative colitis I had been diagnosed with as a toddler. I remember feeling ashamed and afraid to come out of the bathroom, as if everyone else knew what was going on with me.

From that point on I became more concerned about my stomach than the moment I was in or the people I was with. That moment and those fears took away my ability to enjoy the present. If my class was going on a field trip, I worried about where the closest bathroom would be instead of anticipating the adventure we were taking. When my family took trips to Disney World, I concentrated on the map to find the nearest bathroom instead of deciding which ride to go on next. I learned to carry extra clothes everywhere I went. At one point, my medical issues got so bad my mother put a potty training portable toilet in the back of our minivan. Our whole life became consumed with stomachaches, diarrhea, and restrictive eating. I had to analyze every menu I looked at and everything I ate. I planned everything around a bathroom and had to restrict how much I hung out with my friends to avoid an embarrassing moment. My entire world revolved around a sickness I never wanted. I began to loathe the diagnosis.

Fear invaded my every thought. In elementary school, I missed recess. I couldn't play kickball or tetherball. My stomach made weird noises and I'd see the kids lean over and whisper to each other. I developed a fear of not being accepted, thinking, "I'm weird, I'm different." In middle school, that fear only got worse.

At that age, image is everything. I was afraid everyone would think of me as the "poopy pants girl". I feared not being accepted, was petrified of another messy accident, and worried I'd miss school because of a long hospital stay.

In high school, I missed most of my sophomore year because of extreme stomach pain. That first month of my sophomore year, I went to the bathroom five times in my first period class. I had so many incidents that I started having panic attacks on the way to school. I figured out how to make it through half the day by eating less and hiding out in the television production department working on "projects". The doctors prescribed heavy doses of UC medication, which caused weight gain and made my energy levels almost nonexistent.

My senior year of high school, the doctors told me my latest colon biopsy showed pre-cancerous cells. They recommended that my large intestines be removed. I was so angry at God and at what such a drastic surgery would do to my life. Doctors reassured me that I could have a successful future but all I saw was more things to be afraid of: scarring, infertility issues, and the possibility of a permanent illium pouch. The answer to all my overwhelming pain was in a surgery that would remove my colon and cure me of colitis, but I'd let fear keep me trapped in stomach pain for so long that I refused the surgery.

All that fear also stirred up a lot of anger toward God. I acted out by making very poor choices in the men I dated. I was looking for acceptance and, the way I saw it, as long as they accepted me there was nothing to be afraid of. The more accepted I felt, the further from God I got.

When I graduated high school, it was decision time—not just to choose a college and future career, but to either put life on hold for surgery or eventually die. One day, it finally hit me: *What did I fear more—death or a large scar and possible colostomy bag?* I realized I feared death more. The Bible says there is no fear in death, yet in that moment I was petrified at the thought of dying—a great indicator that my heart was not right with God. I feared standing before a righteous God and trying to explain why I squandered my life on idle things like dating relationships, vengeful gossip, and destructive friendships.

In the summer of 2001, I started the long process of having my large intestines removed. I got over my fear and allowed doctors to fix my body. However, the journey to fix the consequences left behind by years of overwhelming fear was just beginning.

Fear is Not an Emotion

Fear has a way of silencing our voice, crushing our dreams, and distancing us from God. It can enter our lives through words or events. For me, a simple experience in a bathroom and words spoken by a stranger were enough for the devil to plant a thought in my mind. The first thing we need to understand about fear is that it's not an emotion; it's not part of our human design from God. Fear is a demonic spirit, meant to distance us from God and prevent us from trusting that God is on our side. The Bible says, *"For the Spirit God gave us does not make us timid"* (2 Timothy 1:7) because God gives us the Holy Spirit!

When Jesus conquered death and the grave, He stripped darkness of its power and *gave it to us*. Jesus has given us power over unclean spirits, and one of those unclean spirits is the spirit of fear. (Mark 6:7 & Luke 9:1 & Luke 10:19)

As believers and followers of Jesus, we have power over every evil thing that comes at us including our fear. **Recognizing the authority and power you possess as a Christ follower is the key to breaking the hold fear has on us**. There are several verses to turn to when you need a reminder of that:

> *Calling the Twelve to Him, He began to send them out two by two and gave them authority over impure spirits.* (Mark 6:7)

> *When Jesus had called the Twelve together, He gave them power and authority to drive out all demons and to cure diseases.* (Luke 9:1)

> *I have given you authority to trample on snakes and scorpions and to overcome all the power of the enemy; nothing will harm you.* (Luke 10:19)

We have to recognize that fear is an evil spirit trying to force its opinion on us. Our goal is to enforce the opinion of God by using the spirit He gave us: "*power, love, and self-discipline.*" (2 Timothy 1:7)

Let Your Faith Be Stronger than Your Fear

People who have been traumatized in life often live in fear long after the trauma has passed. For them, fear has become normal in their life. The trauma could be an accident, or poverty, or a troubled marriage—there's a variety of events that evoke fear and inject worried thoughts into every situation. Those derailing thoughts are meant to divide your relationship with your Creator and distance you from God's healing power.

Fear may seem to have a name and a voice but give it no place in your life. Jesus has provided us everything we need to overcome fear. Peace must counter every thought of fear that enters our minds. If we understand that fear's purpose is to separate us from everything we have in God, we can start recognizing fear when we hear it speaking in our minds.

Life is choice-driven. We can choose to walk in fear or we can choose to have faith. Fear is a tool used by the Devil to destroy our relationship with God. Peace is the weapon Jesus provided to us when He died on the cross and rose again. It is up to us to decide which weapon we will use to have victory in our lives.

It is easy to believe in things we see, but it takes faith to believe something you have never seen before. When we are confronted with negativity, whatever the situation may be, it's easy for a spirit of fear to begin its intimidation. When I did not see healing in my body, it was hard to have faith that God was on my side and that God wanted me to experience a pain-free life. Walking by faith means we keep moving forward, regardless of the struggles, always trusting in God. He will erase our fear if we put our faith in Him.

Questions for Reflection

1. What is your biggest fear?

2. What comes to mind when you begin thinking about that fear?

3. How much of your time is spent thinking about a situation that causes fear?

4. Have you prayed and asked God to help you with the thing or circumstance you fear?

5. Read Mark 6:7 and Luke 9:1. Do you believe God has given us power over unclean spirits? Does this include fear?

6. Find three scriptures about peace you can use to combat fear in your life.

About the Authors

Lena Meadowcroft

> *Trust in the Lord with all your heart,*
> *And lean not on your own understanding;*
> *In all your ways acknowledge Him,*
> *And He shall direct your paths.*
>
> Proverbs 3:5-6

Lena Meadowcroft and her husband Michael started their North Tampa church, ASAP Church, in February 2016, with the dream of connecting the modern family to a relationship with Jesus. Prior to starting the church, they both worked with other church pastors. Lena helped launch a Christian satellite network and worked with middle and high school students in various youth ministries in Florida, Texas, and California. She grew up in Tampa and Ocala, Florida, and attended college at the University of Miami. Before working in ministry, Lena spent ten years working in television media as a news producer. She's written news copy and produced news coverage for stories like the terror attacks on 9/11, hurricanes Charley and Katrina, and the presidential elections in 2004 and 2008.

Lena was diagnosed with ulcerative colitis when she was four years old. This helped shape her relationship with Jesus. She struggled as a teen to trust God with her illness, which caused her to push away from God and seek fulfillment in other relationships. A college classmate invited her to church just before college graduation, and she found herself repenting to God and asking Jesus to take over her life. While working in television, God spoke to Lena to return to school to earn a Master's degree in Ministerial Leadership at Southeastern University.

She is a bonus mom of a stepson, Michael, and two Maltese dogs named Miracle and Faith. When she is not working on church business, she enjoys spending time with her husband and watching movies.

Lucy Kyllonen

Being confident of this very thing, that He who has begun a good work in you (me) will complete it until the day of Jesus Christ.
                             Philippians 1:6

Lucy Kyllonen has been in urban ministry alongside her husband, for over twenty years at Crossover Church in Tampa, Florida. She has served in a variety of positions from Youth Ministry, to conference and retreat planning, church administration, and currently serves as the Director of C.H.O.S.E.N. Women's ministry. Her roles include teaching, speaking, leading, and mentoring at different levels. Lucy holds a BA in Psychology from Southeastern University and an MA in Mental Health Counseling from The University of South Florida. She has a passion to see women of all backgrounds empowered to reach their God-given potential and to live extraordinary lives. Lucy enjoys reading, sleeping, nature walks, and spending time with her husband and her two daughters. To follow Lucy on Facebook, Instagram or Twitter you can find her at @lucyk813.

www.ingramcontent.com/pod-product-compliance
Lightning Source LLC
Chambersburg PA
CBHW070606010526
44118CB00012B/1453